VOGUE

CLASSIC CROCHET

VOGUE

CLASSIC CROCHET

ANNE MATTHEWS

PHOTOGRAPHY BY
CLIVE ARROWSMITH

PYRAMID BOOKS

Particular thanks are due,
for his special contribution,
to Vogue *stylist Bill Reed*

This edition published in 1989 by Pyramid Books,
an imprint of the Octopus Publishing Group,
Michelin House, 81 Fulham Road, London SW3 6RB.

© The Condé Nast Publications Limited 1989
ISBN 1 871307 74 0
Produced by Mandarin Offset
printed in Hong Kong

contents

·introduction·

VOGUE published its renowned knitting books from the 1930s through to the 1970s. In many ways it was the forerunner in its field – the first to show designs in colour, the first to show fashionable styles, not just garments. Although the twice yearly books were called *Vogue Knitting Book*, they also featured crochet and it is from the archive copies of these books that the patterns for this book have been selected.

In recent years crochet hasn't enjoyed the high profile accorded to knitwear but it is equally as versatile and stylish and as simple. Crochet relies on a few basic stitches which are easily learnt and all pattern stitches are worked from these. There are many interesting stitches, each giving a different texture, a different look to the finished work; all are well suited to the making of good-looking, fashionable clothes. The aim of the book has been throughout to show crochet in stylish form, not in the sense of designs that will be out of fashion before they are finished, but as contemporary classics to wear and wear again.

You don't have to be an expert: there are patterns for beginners as well as patterns for the more experienced crocheter, and the Techniques section at the end of the book has clear line drawings showing just how each basic stitch is worked.

Because crochet is worked to tension in the same way as knitting, once the right stitch and yarn have been found, it is simple to convert a knitting pattern to crochet. To prove the point, a number of the designs were, originally, knitted but have been successfully adapted to crochet. Do, please, always work a tension square first as the instructions will only work to the given measurements if your tension is the same as in the instructions. Remember too that if you lengthen any of the designs, more yarn may be needed.

Crochet can also be used to add style to a plain knit as an edging round a twinset, a lacy inset at the neck of a dress, and as the front bands and cuffs of a shapely cardigan blouse. Continuing the theme of versatility, some designs are finished with knitted ribs at cuffs and hem while others obtain the same effect with a crocheted rib.

ANNE MATTHEWS

WAFFLE PATTERN SWEATER

1984

* *Originally made in stocking stitch, this loose-fitting grandpa vest has been re-worked in a more stylish raised waffle stitch. Knitted ribs are used to edge the pocket, cuffs and welts*

MATERIALS.—Pingouin Corrida 3: 15 50 g balls; pair of 3 mm (11) and 3¾ mm (9) needles; 4 mm (8) crochet hook; 6 buttons.
TENSION.—24 sts and 28 rows to 10 cm [4 inches] over pattern stitch 1.
STITCHES.—1. Waffle pattern; 2. st.st; 3. k1, p1 twisted rib; 4. k2, p2 rib.
SIZE.—To fit bust 92 cm [36 inches]. Actual measurement 104 cm [44 inches]; length 77.5 cm [30½ inches]; sleeve seam 53.5 cm [21 inches].
ABBREVIATIONS.—alt-alternate; beg-beginning; ch-chain; cont-continue; dec-decrease; foll-following; inc-increase; k-knit; rem-remaining; rep-repeat; rf/tr-yarn round hook, hook from front from right to left round stem of stitch and complete in usual way; sl.st-slip st; st(s)-stitch(es); tr-treble; yrh-yarn round hook.

BACK.—With 4 mm (8) hook make a loose ch of 127, yrh, hook into 4th ch from hook and work 1 tr in this and all subsequent ch to end of row, 2 turning ch. This is the foundation row.
row 1: miss first st, * 1 rf/tr in each next 2 sts, 1 tr in next st; rep from * to end of row ending with 1 tr in turning ch, 2 turning ch.
row 2: miss first st, * 1 tr in each next 2 sts, 1 rf/tr in next st; rep from * to end of row ending with 1 tr in turning ch, 2 turning ch. These two rows form pattern.
Cont in pattern until work measures 37 cm [14½ inches] ending with right side facing.
SHAPE ARMHOLES.—Sl.st across first 9 sts, work in pattern to last 9 sts and turn. Work on these 105 sts for a further 27 rows.
SHAPE BACK NECK.—With right side facing, work 45 sts and turn. Work on these sts for first side, dec 1 st at neck edge on every row until 34 sts remain.
Fasten off.
Leave centre 15 sts, rejoin yarn to rem sts and complete to match first side, reversing all shapings.
POCKET LINING.—With 3¾ mm (9) needles, cast on 21 sts and work in st.st for 10 cm [4 inches].
Cast off loosely.

FRONT.—Work as for Back to armhole shapings.
SHAPE ARMHOLES, PLACE POCKET LINING AND DIVIDE FOR FRONT

OPENING.—With right side facing, sl.st across first 9 sts for armhole, work 13 sts in pattern, then work 21 sts from pocket lining in pattern, miss next 21 sts on body, work 15 sts, turn and cont on these 49 sts. Work in pattern for 27 rows.

SHAPE FRONT NECK.—Work 43 sts, turn and cont on rem sts, dec 1 st at neck edge on every alt row until 34 sts rem. Cont in pattern until work measures same as Back.

Fasten off.

Miss centre 7 sts for Front Opening and cont on rem 58 sts. Work to match first side of Front omitting pocket.

FRONT BORDERS.—(Button Border) With 3 mm (11) needles, cast on 7 sts and work in k1, p1 twisted rib (k into back of all k sts) until border fits neatly up front opening, slightly stretched.

Mark position for 5 buttons on this border, the first to come on the 5th row and the others spaced evenly between allowing for 6th button in neckband.

(Buttonhole Border) With 3 mm (11) needles pick up and rib 7 sts from centre front. Work in twisted rib as for button border working buttonholes opposite marked positions as follows: rib 2 sts, yarn round needle, k2 tog, rib to end.

NECK EDGE.—Join shoulder seams. With 3 mm (11) needles and right side facing, pick up and rib 7 sts from border, knit 6 sts up right front neck, 41 sts side front, 1 st at shoulder seam, 11 sts down side back, 15 sts centre back, 11 sts up side back, 1 st at shoulder seam, 41 sts down side front, 6 sts at front neck and rib 7 sts from border. Work in twisted rib for 7 rows working a buttonhole

on the 4th row to match others.

Cast off loosely ribwise.

POCKET TOP.—With 3 mm (11) needles and right side facing, pick up and knit 21 sts along pocket top. Work in twisted rib for 7 rows.

Cast off ribwise.

SLEEVES.—With 4 mm (8) hook make a loose ch of 53, yrh, hook into 4th ch from hook and work 1 tr in this and all subsequent ch to end of row, 2 turning ch. Cont in pattern as for Back inc 1 st at each end of every 3rd row until there are 129 sts, cont in pattern until work measures 44.5 cm [$17\frac{1}{2}$ inches] ending with right side facing.

SHAPE TOP.—Sl.st across first 9 sts, work to last 9 sts.

Fasten off.

WELTS.—(worked separately) With 3 mm (11) needles and right side facing, pick up and knit 108 sts evenly across base chain. Work in k2, p2 rib for 9 cm [$3\frac{1}{2}$ inches].

Cast off loosely ribwise.

CUFFS.—With 3 mm (11) needles and right side facing, pick up and knit 52 sts evenly along base chain. Work in k2, p2 rib for 9 cm [$3\frac{1}{2}$ inches].

Cast off loosely ribwise.

TO MAKE UP.—Sew pocket lining and pocket top into place. Set sleeves into place, centre of sleeve to shoulder seam and the rest set evenly each side, sew into place, sew side and sleeve seams. Sew buttons to match buttonholes.

See ball band for pressing instructions.

CROCHET BAND BLOUSE

1951

* A close-fitting cardigan blouse knitted in stocking stitch with contrast bands striped in double crochet edging the three quarter length sleeves, the fronts and V-neckline

MATERIALS.—Wendy Ascot 4 ply: 7(7:8:8:9) 50 g balls Main colour; 1(1:1:2:2) 50 g balls Contrast colour; 3 mm (11) crochet hook; pair of 3 mm (11) knitting needles; 6 buttons.

TENSION.—16 sts and 20 rows to 5 cm [2 inches] over st. 1

STITCHES.—1. stocking stitch; 2. double crochet.

SIZES.—To fit bust size 81(86:91:96:102) cm [32(34:36:38:40) inches]. Actual measurements: 89(94:99:104:109) cm [35(37:39:41:43) inches]; length to shoulder 51(53.5:54.5:55:57) cm [20(20¾:21½:21¾:22½) inches]; sleeve seam with cuff 33(34:34:35.5:35.5) cm [13(13½:13½:14:14) inches].

Figures in brackets () refer to larger sizes.

ABBREVIATIONS.—beg-begin(ing); C-Contrast colour; ch-chain; dc-double crochet; dec-decrease; inc-increase; k-knit; M-Main colour; p-purl; rep-repeat; st.st-stocking stitch; st(s)-stitch(es).

BACK.—With M and 3 mm (11) needles cast on 112(120:128:136:144) sts. Work 2.5 cm [1 inch] in st.st ending with a k row. K next row to mark hemline. Work 10 rows. Dec 1 st each end of next and every 6th row until 100(108:116:124:132) sts remain.

Work until Back measures 14 cm [5½ inches] from hemline ending with a p row. Inc 1 st each end of next and every 4th row until there are 136(144:152:160:168) sts. Work until Back measures 33(34:35.5:35.5:37) cm [13(13½:14:14:14½) inches] from hemline or desired length to armholes.

SHAPE ARMHOLES.—Cast off 7(8:9:10:11) sts at beg of next 2 rows. Dec 1 st each end of every k row until 108(112:116:120:124) sts remain. Work until armholes are 18(18.5:19:19.5:20.5) cm [7(7¼:7½:7¾:8) inches] measured on the straight.

SHAPE SHOULDERS.—Cast off at beg of next and following rows 8(9:9:9:9) sts 6 times and 9(7:8:9:10) sts twice.

Cast off remaining 42(44:46:48:50) sts.

LEFT FRONT.—With M and 3 mm (11) needles cast on 52(56:60:64:68) sts. Work 2.5 cm [1 inch] ending with a k row. K next row to mark hemline. Work 10 rows. Dec 1 st at beg of next and every 6th row until 46(50:54:58:62) sts remain. Work until Front measures 14 cm [5½ inches] from hemline ending with a p row. Inc 1 st at beg of next and every 4th row until there are 64(68:72:76:80) sts. Work until Front measures same as Back to armholes ending with a p row.

SHAPE ARMHOLE.—Cast off 7(8:9:10:11) sts at beg of next row. Dec 1 st at same edge every k row until 50(52:54:56:58) sts remain.

*Bands of double
crochet in a
contrasting colour add
a stylish finish to this
classic cardigan*

Work until armhole is 13(14:14:15:15) cm [5(5½:5½:6:6) inches] measured on the straight ending with a k row.
SHAPE NECK.—Cast off at this edge 3(4:5:6:7) sts once and 2 sts seven times. Work until armhole measures same as that for Back.
SHAPE SHOULDERS.—Cast off at this edge 8(9:9:9:9) sts three times and 9(7:8:9:10) sts once.

RIGHT FRONT.—Follow instructions for Left Front reading k for p and p for k and reversing shapings.

SLEEVES.—With M and 3 mm (11) needles cast on 78(82:84:88:92) sts. Work 8 rows. Inc 1 st at each end of next and every 8th row

until there are 100(104:108:112:116) sts. Work until sleeve measures 27(28:28:29:29) cm [10½(11:11:11½:11½) inches] or 6 cm [2½ inches] less than desired sleeve length.
SHAPE TOP.—Cast off 6(7:8:9:10) sts at beg of next 2 rows. Dec 1 st each end of next 5 rows then every k row until 44 sts remain. Cast off 4 sts at beg of next 6 rows.
Cast off.

TO MAKE UP.—Sew shoulder seams. Set in sleeves. Sew side and sleeve seams. Turn up and slip stitch hem.

EDGING.—With 3 mm (11) hook and M join yarn to lower right front edge.
row 1: with right side of work facing, work 1 row of dc along right front, neck, and left front edge.
row 2: join C at right front, work to neck edge, 2 dc in corner st, work round neck, 2 dc in corner st, work down left front.
row 3: as row 2
row 4: as row 2 but using M.
Rep last 3 rows always starting at right front and working 2 rows in C, 1 row in M alternately to end of second C stripe.
WORK BUTTONHOLES.—next row: work 2(2.5:3:4:5) cm [¾(1:1¼:1½:2) inches], * 2 ch, miss 2 dc, work 5 cm [2 inches]; rep from * 5 times more, work to end.
next row: work a dc in each ch of previous row.
Work to end of fourth C stripe. Sew in all ends.
Work round sleeves in same way working 2 rounds M after fifth C stripe ending with 1 round in M.

FINISHING.—Press work. Sew on buttons. See ball band for pressing instructions.

SCOOP-NECKED BLOUSE

1 9 5 2

** *This close-fitting, scoop-necked blouse in broken shell pattern has the delicate appearance of guipure lace. The kimono sleeves are worked in one piece with the front and back of the blouse*

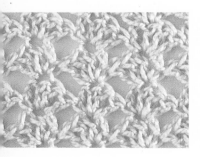

MATERIALS.—Rowan Cable mercerised-cotton: 8(9:10:10) 50 g balls; 3 mm (3) hook.
TENSION.—5 shells to 7.5 [3 inches]; 3 rows to 2.5 cm [1 inch].
STITCH.—1. shell pattern.
SIZES.—To fit bust 81(86:91:96) cm [32(34:36:38) inches]. Actual measurements: 85(91:98:103) cm [33½(36:38½:40½) inches]; length 52 cm [20½ inches].
Figures in brackets () refer to larger sizes.
ABBREVIATIONS.—ch-chain; cont-continue; dc-double crochet; dec-decrease; inc-increase; patt-pattern; rep-repeat; st(s)-stitch(es); tr-treble; yrh-yarn round hook.

BACK.—With 3 mm (3) hook, make 115(123:131:139) ch, yrh,1 tr in 3rd ch from hook, 1 ch, * 1 dc in next ch, 2 ch, 3 tr in same ch, miss 3 ch; rep from * ending with 1 tr in last ch, 2 turning ch.
This is the foundation row.
row 1: 1 tr in tr, * (1 dc, 2 ch, 3 tr) in top of 3rd tr of each shell patt rep from * ending with 1 tr in turning ch, 2 turning ch. 28(30:32:34) shells.
This row forms pattern.
Work 4 rows.
Dec 1 shell at each end of next and every fourth row until there are 20(22:24:26) shells.
Work 4 rows.
Inc 1 shell at each end of next and every fourth row until there are 28(30:32:34) shells.
BEGIN SLEEVES.— Inc 1 shell at end of each next ten rows. 38(40:42:44) shells. Work 37 ch at end of last row.
row 11: work 9 shells over these ch, work in patt to end, work 37 ch.
repeat this row twice more.
row 14: work 9 shells over 37 ch, work to end. 74(76:78:80) shells. **
Work 15 rows
SHAPE NECK AND SLEEVES.—row 1: work 33(34:35:36) shells, turn. Finish this side first.
row 2: sl.st over first shell, 2 ch, work to last 5 shells, turn.
row 3: sl.st over 4 shells, work to last shell, 2 turning ch.
row 4: sl.st over first shell, 2 ch, work to last 4 shells, turn. 17(18:19:20) shells.
Keeping neck edge straight, cont to decrease 4 shells on each next row until 5(6:7:8) shells remain.
next row: dec 1 shell at shoulder edge, work to end.
Fasten off. Leave 8 shells at centre for neck, rejoin yarn and work to match other side.

FRONT.—Work as for Back to **
Work 4(4:5:5) more rows ending at sleeve

edge to start shaping.

SHAPE NECK.—Work 35(36:37:38) shells.
Turn. Sl.st over next shell, work to end.

next row: work to last shell, turn.

next row: sl.st over first shell, work to end.
Continue dec at neck edge until there are
30(31:32:33) shells.

Continue straight until 15 rows for sleeve
edge have been worked.

next row: work to last 5 shells of sleeve, turn.

row 1: sl.st over next 4 shells, work to end.

row 2: work to last 4 shells, turn.

Repeat these two rows until 5(6:7:8) shells are
left.

Dec 1 shell at sleeve edge, work to end.
Fasten off.

Leave 4 shells at centre for neck, rejoin yarn
and work to match first side.

TO MAKE UP.—Sew shoulder seams, leaving
5 shells open at each edge. Sew side and sleeve
seams. Work 1 row of shells around neck edge.

SHAWL-COLLARED SWEATER

1956

*** Shawl-collared, long sleeved sweater worked in a soft blend of wool, acrylic and mohair. Alternating relief trebles giving a rib effect. The welts, cuffs and collar are knitted in rib*

MATERIALS.—Pingouin Confort: 18(19:20:21:22) 50 g balls; 4 mm (8) crochet hook; pair of 3¼ mm (10) knitting needles.

TENSION.—20 sts and 12 rows to 10 cm [4 inches] over stitch 1.

STITCHES.—1. relief trebles; 2. k1, p1 rib.

SIZES.—To fit chest 91(97:102:107:112) cm [36(38:40:42:44) inches]. Actual measurement 97(102:107:112:117) cm [38(40:42:44:46) inches]; length from shoulder 63.5(63.5:63.5:66:66) cm [25(25:25:26:26) inches]; sleeve seam 47 cm [18½ inches].

Figures in brackets () refer to larger sizes.

ABBREVIATIONS.—alt-alternate; beg-beginning; ch-chain; cont-continue; dec-decrease; foll-following; inc-increase; k-knit; p-purl; rb/tr-yarn round hook, hook from behind and right to left round the stem of stitch and complete in usual way; rem-remaining; rep-repeat; rf/tr-yarn round hook, hook from front from right to left round stem of stitch and complete in usual way; sl.st-slip stitch; st(s)-stitch(es); tr-treble; yrh-yarn round hook.

BACK.—With 4 mm (8) hook, make 98(103:108:113:118) ch, yrh, hook in 3rd ch from hook and work 1 tr in this and all subsequent ch to end of row, turn.

This is the foundation row.

row 1: 2 ch [counts as one tr], miss first st, * 1 rf/tr in next st, 1 rb/tr round next st; rep from * ending with 1 tr in turning ch. turn.

Row 1 forms pattern. Cont in pattern until work measures 58.5(58.5:58.5:61:61) cm [23(23:23:24:24) inches] ending with right side facing.

SHAPE SHOULDERS.—Sl.st across first 14(15:16:17:19) sts, pattern to last 14(15:16:17:19) sts and turn.

Sl.st across first 14(15:16:17:19) sts, pattern to last 14(15:16:17;19) sts.

Fasten off.

FRONT.—Work as for Back until work measures 35(35:35:37.5:37.5) cm [14(14:14:14¾:14¾) inches] ending with right side facing.

SHAPE NECK.—Keeping pattern correct work 40(42:45:47:51) sts and turn.

Work on these sts for first side, dec 1 st at neck edge on next and every foll alt row until 28(30:32:34:38) sts rem, cont in pattern until work measures same as Back to shoulder, ending with right side facing.

SHAPE SHOULDERS.—Sl.st across first 14(15:16:17:19) sts, pattern to end.

Fasten off.

Rejoin yarn to rem sts, sl.st across first 16(17:16:17:16) sts, work on rem sts to match first side.

SLEEVES.—With 4 mm (8) hook, make 56 ch

and work in pattern as on body, at the same time and keeping pattern correct, inc 1 st at each end of every alt row until there are 100 sts.

Cont in pattern until work measures 42 cm [16¼ inches].

Fasten off.

WELTS.—(worked separately) With 3¼ mm (10) needles and right side facing, pick up and k 96(101:106:111:116) sts evenly along base ch, dec 10(11:10:11:10) sts evenly across first row, work in k1, p1 rib for 5 cm [2 inches]. Cast off ribwise allowing for natural ease.

CUFFS.—With 3¼ mm (10) needles and right side facing, pick up and k 54 sts evenly along base chain, dec 4 sts evenly across first row, work in k1, p1 rib for 5 cm [2 inches].
Cast off ribwise allowing for natural ease.

NECKBAND AND COLLAR.—Join shoulder seam.

With 3¼ mm (10) needles and right side facing, pick up and k approx 56 sts up right front neck, 42 sts across back neck, 56 sts down left front neck, work in k1, p1 rib for 16 cm [6½ inches].

Cast off loosely ribwise.

TO MAKE UP.—Fold collar in half and sl.st into place without pulling tight. Set sleeves into place, centre of sleeve to shoulder seam and the rest set evenly each side, sew into place. Sew sleeve and side seams.

See ball band for pressing instructions.

CROCHET TABARD

1966

** *A simply shaped tabard uses a combination of clusters and picots for texture. The two side tabs are worked in half trebles and are fastened with crochet covered buttons*

MATERIALS.—Twilley's Stalite: 9(9:10:10) 50 g balls; 3 mm (10) crochet hook; 4 crocheted buttons.
TENSION.—5 clusters and 3 rows of clusters (6 rows) to 5 cm [2 inches].
STITCHES.—1. half trebles; 2. cluster pattern; 3. double crochet.

SIZES.—To fit bust 81(86:91:97) cm [32(34: 36:38) inches]. Actual measurements 85(91: 97:103) cm [$33\frac{1}{2}$(36:$38\frac{1}{2}$:$40\frac{3}{4}$) inches]; length 62(62:62:62) cm [$24\frac{1}{2}$($24\frac{1}{2}$:$24\frac{1}{2}$:$24\frac{1}{2}$) inches]. Figures in brackets () refer to larger sizes.
ABBREVIATIONS.—ch-chain; cont-continue; dc-double crochet; htr-half treble; patt-pattern; rep-repeat; picot-5 ch, sl.st in 5th ch from hook; sl.st-slip stitch; tr-treble; yrh-yarn round hook

FRONT.—With 3 mm (10) hook, make a loose ch of 85(91:97:103), yrh, hook into 3rd ch from hook and work 1 htr in this and all subsequent ch to end of row, 3 turning ch.
row 1: work 2 htr in 2nd htr of previous row, leaving the last loop of each tr on hook, yrh and draw through all loops on hook [a cluster formed], 1 picot, * miss next htr, work 1 cluster in next htr, 1 picot; rep from * to end with last cluster in turning ch and omitting the picot at end of last rep, 2 turning ch.
row 2: 1 htr in first cluster, * keeping picot in front of work, work 2 htr in top of next cluster; rep from * to last cluster, 1 htr in last cluster, 1 htr in turning ch, 3 turning ch.
These 2 rows form pattern.
Work straight until work measures 41 cm [16 inches] ending with row 1 of pattern and 1 turning ch.
SHAPE ARMHOLES.—row 1: sl.st in first cluster, 1 ch, sl.st in 2nd cluster, 1 ch, sl.st in 3rd cluster, 1 ch, * keeping picot in front of work, work 2 htr in top of next cluster; rep from * until 3 clusters remain, 1 turning ch.
row 2: sl.st in each of first 2 htr, 3 ch, 1 cluster, 1 picot in next htr, cont in patt until 2 htr remain and omit picot at end of last rep, 1 turning ch.
row 3: sl.st in first cluster, 1 ch, * keeping picot in front of work, work 2 htr in top of each cluster until 1 cluster remains, 3 turning ch.
Cont in patt until front measures 52 cm[($20\frac{1}{2}$ inches] ending with row 1 of patt.

SHAPE NECK.—row 1: work over 14(15:16:17) clusters, 2 turning ch. Do not make a picot in last cluster.

row 2: sl.st in first cluster, 1 ch, sl.st in 2nd cluster, 1 ch, 2 htr in next cluster, cont in patt to end, 2 turning ch.

row 3: as row 1 of patt over 12(13:14:15) clusters omitting the picot in the last rep, 1 tr in turning ch, 2 turning ch.

row 4: 2 htr in next cluster, cont in patt to end, 3 turning ch.

row 5: as row 1 of patt over 11(12:13:14) clusters, 2 turning ch.

row 6: as row 4.

row 7: as row 1 of patt over 10(11:12:13) clusters, 2 turning ch.

row 8: as row 4.

row 9: as row 1 of patt over 9(10:11:12) clusters, 1 tr in turning ch, 2 turning ch.

row 10: work over 6(7:8:9) clusters, 3 turning ch.

row 11: work cluster in 3rd htr, cont in patt to end, 2 turning ch.

row 12: work htr over shaped edge to end. Fasten off.

Rejoin yarn in top of 14(15:16:17) cluster from other armhole edge and work to match.

BACK.—Work as for Front omitting the neck shaping until Back measures same as Front to shoulder.

SHAPE NECK.—Starting with the 1st patt row, sl.st over 3(4:5:6) clusters, work over 5 clusters, turn and work in htr to armhole edge.

Rejoin yarn in 9(10:11:12)th cluster from armhole edge, turn. Work over 5 clusters, 1 htr, 1 sl.st in next, turn and work back in htr.

TO MAKE UP.—Join shoulder seams and work 2 rows of dc evenly around the neck edge. Then work 2 rows of dc evenly around armhole edges. Join the side seams for 8 rows from armhole. Work 2 rows of dc down each side and across the Front and Back edges.

TABS.—(work two) With 3 mm (10) hook make 14 ch, yrh, put hook in third ch from hook and work 1 htr in this and all subsequent ch to end of row, 2 turning ch.

row 1: 1 htr in each htr to end, 2 turning ch.

row 2: 1 htr in each next 5 htr, 2 ch, miss 2 htr, work to end, 2 turning ch.

row 3: 1 htr in each next 5 htr, 2 htr in 2 ch space, work to end, 2 turning ch.

Cont in htr until Tab is 16.5 cm [6½ inches]. Do not break off yarn but cont round the outside edges, working 2 dc rows.

Fasten off. Sew in all ends. Sew on buttons.

CROCHET CARDIGAN

1952

* A loose-fitting cardigan with kimono sleeves is
worked in a mercerised cotton and simple openwork
arch stitch pattern. The cuffs and welts are in a knitted
rib

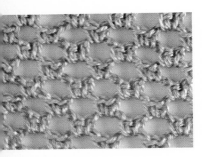

MATERIALS.—Pingouin Fil D'Ecosse no.
4: 11(12:13:14) 50 g balls; 3.50 mm (9) crochet
hook; pair of $3\frac{1}{4}$ mm (10) knitting needles; 9
buttons.
TENSION.—24 sts and 16 rows to 10 cm [4
inches] over stitch 1.
STITCHES.—1. openwork stitch; 2. k1, p1
rib.
SIZES.—To fit bust 81(86:91:97) cm
[32(34:36:38) inches]. Actual measurements
89(94:99:104) cm [35(37:39:41) inches];
length 55(55:61:61) cm [$21\frac{3}{4}$($21\frac{3}{4}$:$24\frac{1}{4}$:$24\frac{1}{4}$)
inches]; sleeve seam 45 cm [18 inches].
Figures in brackets () refer to larger sizes.

ABBREVIATIONS.—alt-alternate; beg-
beginning; ch-chain; ch sp-chain space; cont-
continue; dc-double crochet; dec-decrease;
foll-following; htr-half treble; inc-increase; k-
knit; p-purl; rem-remaining; rep-repeat; sl-
slip; sl.st-slip stitch; st(s)-stitch(es); tbl-
through back of loop; tog-together; yrh-yarn
round hook; yrn-yarn round needle.

BACK.—With 3.50 mm (9) hook make
98(102:106:110) ch, yrh, hook into second ch
and work 1 dc in this and next ch, * 3 ch, miss
2 ch, 1 dc in each next 2 ch; repeat from * to
end, 4 turning ch. This is the foundation row.
row 1: * 2 dc in centre of 3 ch arch, 3 ch; rep
from * ending with 2 dc, 1 htr in first dc of
previous row, 1 turning ch.
row 2: 1 dc in first htr, 1 dc in ch space, * 3 ch,
2 dc in 3 ch arch; rep from * ending with 2 dc,
4 turning ch.
Rows 1 & 2 form pattern.
Continue in pattern until work measures
25(25:27.5:27.5) cm [10(10:11:11) inches]
ending with right side facing.
SLEEVES.—Now keeping pattern correct,
ch 6 sts at beg of next 18 rows then cont in
pattern until work measures 47(47:53:53) cm
[$18\frac{1}{2}$($18\frac{1}{2}$:21:21) inches] ending with right side
facing.
SHAPE SHOULDERS.—Sl.st across first 54
sts, pattern to last 54 sts, turn with 1 turning
ch, sl.st across next 14(15:16:17) sts, turn,
pattern to last 14(15:16:17) sts, turn, work 1
row, sl.st across 15(16:17:18) sts, pattern to
last 15(16:17:18) sts.
Fasten off.

LEFT FRONT.—With 3.50 mm (9) hook
make 48(50:52:54) ch and work as for Back
until work measures 25(25:27:27) cm
[10(10:11:11) inches], ending at side edge.
SLEEVE AND FRONT SHAPING.—Now
keeping pattern correct, ch 6 sts at side edge
on next and every foll alt row 9 times (54 sts
added). **At the same time**, dec 1 st at front

Ribbed welts add definition to this pretty loose-fitting cardigan

edge on next and every foll alt row 20 times, cont in pattern until work measures same as Back to shoulder, ending with right side facing.

SHAPE SHOULDER.—Sl.st across first 54 sts, pattern to end, turn, pattern to last 14(15:16:17) sts, turn, sl.st across first 15(16:17:18) sts, pattern to end.
Fasten off.

RIGHT FRONT.—Work as for Left Front reversing all shapings.

WELTS.—(Back) With 3¼ mm (10) needles and right side facing, pick up and k 98(102:106:110) sts evenly along base chain.

Working in k1, p1 rib, dec 10 sts evenly across first row. Cont in rib for 8 cm [3¼ inches].
Cast off ribwise, allowing for natural ease.
(Fronts—both alike) With 3¼ mm (10) needles and right side facing, pick up and k 46(48:50:52) sts. Working in k1, p1 rib, dec 5 sts evenly across first row. Cont in rib for 8 cm [3¼ inches].
Cast off ribwise, allowing for natural ease.
Work other front to match.
(Sleeves) With 3¼ mm (10) needles and right side facing, pick up and k approx 56 sts along base chain. Working in k1, p1 rib, dec 6 sts evenly across first row. Cont in rib for 8 cm [3¼ inches].
Cast off ribwise, allowing for natural ease.

BUTTON BAND.—Join shoulder seams. With 3¼ mm (10) needles, cast on 8 sts and work in k1, p1 rib until band fits neatly up front to centre back neck, slightly stretched. Cast off ribwise.
Mark positions for 9 buttons on this band, the first to come on 3rd row and the last to come 5 cm [2 inches] after start of front shaping, with the others spaced evenly in between.

BUTTONHOLE BAND.—Work as for Button Band, working buttonholes opposite marked positions as follows:
Buttonhole row: rib 3, k2 tog, yrn, rib to end.

TO MAKE UP.—Pin front bands into place, easing to fit. Sew into place with a flat seam. Join with a flat seam at centre back neck. Sew side and sleeve seams, sew buttons to match buttonholes.
See ball band for pressing instructions.

V-NECK SLIPOVER

1932

** Lightweight, slipover worked in an open double arch pattern with knitted ribbed edging. First made in a 2 ply, this contemporary version is in a machine-washable 4 ply Merino wool*

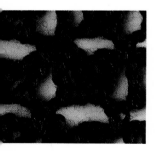

MATERIALS.—Jaeger Matchmaker 4 ply: 5(5:6) 50 g balls; 3 mm (10) crochet hook; pair of 2¾ mm (12) knitting needles.

TENSION.—2 patterns to 1.75 cm [¾ inch] over stitch 2; 4 rows to 4 cm [1½ inches] approximately.

STITCHES.—1. k1, p1 rib; 2. lace pattern.

SIZES.—To fit bust 86–92(96–101:107–112) cm [32–34(36–38:40–42) inches]. Actual measurements: 93(102:111) cm [36½(40¼:43¾) inches]; length 55 cm [21¾ inches].
Figures in brackets () refer to larger sizes.

ABBREVIATIONS.—ch-chain; dec-decrease; dtr-double treble; htr-half treble; k-knit; p-purl; sl.st-slip stitch; st(s)-stitch(es).

BACK.—Cast on 127(139:151) sts with 2¾ mm (12) needles. Work in k1, p1 rib for 6 cm [2¼ inches]. Cast off leaving last loop free. With 3 mm (10) hook, put hook into free loop, 1 ch. Work 1 dc in first st, * 5 ch, miss 5 sts, 1 dc in next st; rep from * to end.

row 1: 1 sl.st in first st, 9 ch, 1 htr in first space, 5 ch, 1 dtr in same space, * (1 dtr, 5 ch, 1 htr, 5 ch, 1 dtr) in next space; rep from * ending with last dtr in dc, 1 turning ch.

row 2: 1 dc in first st, * 5 ch, 1 dc in centre of ch group; rep from * ending with last dc in 4th ch.

Rows 1 & 2 form pattern.

Continue in pattern until work measures 34 cm [13¼ inches] from beginning of work ending with a row 2. **.

SHAPE ARMHOLES.—sl.st across work for 4 cm [1½ inches], continue in pattern to last 4 cm [1½ inches] turn. work 1 row. Sl.st across work for 1.5 cm [½ inch], continue in pattern to last 1.5 cm [½ inch], turn.

Work straight until armhole measures 20 cm [8 inches] ending at armhole edge and with a row 2.

SHAPE SHOULDERS.—work 5 patterns, turn. Work 1 more row.

Fasten off.

Leave rem sts at centre for back of neck. Rejoin yarn to other shoulder and work to match. Fasten off.

FRONT.—Work as for Back to ** but when work measures 31 cm [12¼ inches] divide for neck.

Working one side at a time, dec 1 st at neck edge on every row until work measures 34 cm [13¼ inches] ending at armhole edge.

SHAPE ARMHOLE.—Continuing to dec at neck edge sl.st across work for 4 cm [1½ inches] continue in pattern to end of row. Work next row to last 2.5 cm [1 inch] of work, turn. Work 1 row. Work to last 1.5 cm [½ inch], turn.

Work straight until armhole measures 20 cm [8 inches] continuing to dec at neck edge, then shape shoulder as for Back.

Fasten off.

Rejoin yarn and work second side to match first. Fasten off.

EDGES.—Neckband: Cast on 250 sts with 2¾ mm (12) needles. Work in k1, p1 rib for 2 cm [¾ inch] dec 1 st at each end of every row. Cast off ribwise.

Armholes (work 2): Cast on 180 sts with 2¾ mm (12) needles. Work in k1, p1 rib for 2 cm [¾ inch].

Cast off ribwise.

TO MAKE UP.—Sew side and shoulder seams. Join the ends of neckband to form the V of the neck and sew in place. Join the ends of the armhole strips and sew in place. See ball band for pressing instructions.

MAN'S WAISTCOAT

1949

** *Classic V-necked, shaped waistcoat with four pockets and front points worked in 4 ply wool and a crochet version of fabric stitch. Rows of double crochet define the edges*

MATERIALS.—Jaeger Matchmaker 4 ply: 7(8:9:9) 50 g balls; 3.50 mm (9) and 3 mm (10) crochet hooks; 6 buttons.

TENSION.—7 sts and 8 rows to 2.5 cm [(1 inch].

STITCHES.—1. fabric stitch; 2. double crochet.

SIZES.—To fit chest 97(102:107:112) cm [38(40:42:44) inches]. Actual measurements 99(105:112:117) cm [39(41½:44:46) inches]; length from centre back 51 cm [20 inches].

Figures in brackets () refer to larger sizes.

ABBREVIATIONS.—beg-beginning; ch-chain; cont-continue; dc-double crochet; dec-decrease; inc-increase; rem-remaining; rep-repeat; st(s)-stitch(es); yrh-yarn round hook.

BACK.—With 3.50 mm (9) hook, make 99(105:113:119) ch, yrh, hook in 2nd ch from hook and work a dc in this and all subsequent ch to end. 98(104:112:118) sts.

row 1: 1 dc in first st, * 1 ch, miss 1 st, 1 dc in next st; rep from * ending with 1 dc in each last 2 sts.

row 2: as row 1 but ending with 1 dc in last st. Rows 1 & 2 form pattern.

Work 2 more rows.

Inc 1 st at each side of every 3rd row until there are 122(136:142:150) sts then every 6th row until there are 136(142:150:156) sts.

Work straight until work measures 27 cm [10½ inches].

SHAPE ARMHOLES.—next row: work to last 7(8:9:10) sts and turn.

Rep this row 3 more times. 108(110:114:116) sts.

Work straight until armhole measures 24 cm [9½ inches].

SHAPE SHOULDERS.—next row: work to last 11 sts, turn. Rep this row 5 more times. 12(44:48:50) sts remain.

Fasten off.

POCKET LININGS.—With 3.50 mm (9) hook, make 26 ch, yrh, hook in 2nd ch from hook and work 1 dc in this and all subsequent ch to end. Work in dc and work straight until work measures 7 cm [2¾ inches].

Work three more linings.

RIGHT FRONT.—With 3.50 mm (9) hook, make 7 ch, yrh, hook into 2nd ch from hook and work in patt as given for Back to end. 6 sts.

Inc 1 st at each end of next 6 rows. 18 sts.

Inc 1 st at front edge on each next 11 rows while inc 5(6:7:8) sts five times at side edge of rows 8, 10, 12, 14 and 16, then 8 sts twice at

side edge of rows 18 and 20. 70(75:80:85) sts. Keeping front edge straight, work 3 rows then inc 1 st at side edge on next and following 8th row and when 38 rows from beg of work have been worked, place 1st pocket lining.

Starting at front edge, work 28 sts, then work 4 rows on next 25 sts and fasten off. Join yarn to rem sts and work to side edge.

next row: work to pocket edge, work across sts of pocket lining and then to front edge. Continue to increase 1 st at side edge on each 8th row.

Join 2nd pocket lining in the same way when 26 more rows have been worked.

When there are 78(82:88:92) sts, and work ends at front edge,

SHAPE FRONT EDGE.—next row: dec 1 st at front edge, work to end.

Cont dec 1 st at front edge on every 4th row until work measures 27 cm [10½ inches] at side.

SHAPE ARMHOLES.—Cont to dec at front edge on every 4th row while dec 7(8:9:10) sts at armhole edge on next 2 rows. Then cont to dec at front edge until there are 33 sts, then work armhole straight for 19 cm [7½ inches].

Cont to dec 1 st at front neck edge three more times and inc 1 st at armhole edge on same rows. 33 sts.

Work straight until armhole measures 24 cm [9½ inches] ending at armhole edge.

Sl.st across 11 sts, work to end, turn. Work to last 11 sts, turn. Sl.st across 11 sts.
Fasten off.

LEFT FRONT.—Work as for Right Front reversing shapings.

NOTE: 5(6:7:8) st inc should be worked at beg of rows 9, 11, 13, 15 and 17, 8 st inc on rows 19 and 21.

Work 5 rows after last inc at front edge of point ending at side edge. Work buttonholes as follows: next row: work to last 6 sts, sl.st over 3 sts, work to end.

next row: work 3 sts, 3 ch over sl.sts, work to end.

next row: work to 3 ch, 3 patt sts in 3 ch space, work to end.

Work 5 more button holes spacing them evenly. Last buttonhole should come approximately 3 rows before front edge shaping.

TO MAKE UP.—Sew side and shoulder seams. Sew down pocket linings. With 3.50 mm (9) hook work 1 row of dc along bottom edge. Change to 3 mm (10) hook and work a further dc row.
Fasten off.
Work these same 2 rows around armholes.
Fasten off.
Sew on buttons.
See ball band for pressing instructions.

FRILLED SHIRT

1966

** *A long sleeved blouse in easy-care acrylic is worked in an open alternating V-pattern for the main parts. Openwork frills edge the sleeves and softly frill the neck and front*

MATERIALS.—Twilleys Galaxia 5: 6(7:7:8) 100 g balls; 2 mm (13) crochet hook; 4 buttons.

TENSION.—3 shell patts to 2.5 cm [1 inch] in width, 9 rows to 5 cm [2 inches] in depth.

STITCHES.—1. Shell pattern; 2. Frill for cuff and neck.

SIZES.—To fit bust 81(86:91:97) cm [32(34:36:38) inches]. Actual measurement: 88(91.5:95:98) cm [34½(36:37½:38½) inches]; length at centre back 53(54:54.5:55) cm [21(21¼:21½:21¾ inches]; sleeve seam (without frill) 43 cm [17 inches].

Figures in brackets () refer to larger sizes.

ABBREVIATIONS.—ch-chain; cont-continue; dc-double crochet; inc-increase; patt-pattern; rep-repeat; sl.st-slip stitch; tr-treble; yrh-yarn round hook.

FRONT.—With 2 mm (13) hook make a ch of 106(110:114:118), yrh, put hook into 4th ch from hook,* (1 tr, 1 ch, 1 tr) in next ch, miss 1 ch; repeat from * to end of row, 3 turning ch. This is the foundation row. 52(54:56:58) shells. Start shell pattern.

row 1: * miss first tr and ch, (1 tr, 1 ch, 1 tr) in space between next 2 tr (1 shell made); rep from * ending with (1 tr, 1 ch, 1 tr) in turning ch, 3 turning ch.

This row forms pattern.

Continue in pattern for 55 rows omitting the 3 ch for turning at end of last row.

SHAPE ARMHOLES.—row 1: sl.st in first tr, (1 ch, 1 sl.st in each next 2 tr) twice, 1 ch, 1 sl.st in next tr, 3 ch, cont in pattern work 46(48:50:52) shells, 3 ch, miss next tr and ch, 1 sl.st in next tr, turn.

row 2: sl.st along 3 ch, 3 ch, work 45(47:49:51) shells, 3 ch, miss next tr and ch, 1 sl.st in next tr, turn.

row 3: sl.st along 3 ch, 3 ch, work 44(46:48:50) shells, 3 ch, miss next tr and ch, 1 sl.st in next tr, turn.

row 4: as row 3 but work 43(45:47:49) shells.

row 5: as row 3 but work 42(44:46:48) shells.

row 6: as row 3 but work 41(43:45:47) shells, 1 tr in 3 ch space, 3 ch, turn.

row 7: miss first tr, work 40(42:44:46) shells, 1 tr in 3 ch space, 3 ch, turn.

row 8: miss first tr, work 39(41:43:45) shells, (1 tr, 1 ch, 1 tr) in 3 ch space, 3 ch, turn. 40(42:44:46) shells.**

Work straight in pattern for 18(19:20:21) rows more.

SHAPE NECK.—row 1: work 17(18:18:19) shells, 3 ch, miss next tr and ch, 1 sl.st along next 2 tr, turn.

Cont on these shells.

row 2: sl.st along 3 ch, next tr, ch and tr, 3 ch, cont in patt to end of row.

row 3: work 15(16:16:17) shells, 3 ch, miss next tr and ch, 1 sl.st in next tr, turn.

row 4: sl.st along 3 ch, 3 ch, cont in patt to end of row.

row 5: work 14(15:15:16) shells, 3 ch, miss next tr and ch, 1 sl.st in next tr, turn.

row 6: sl.st along 3 ch, 3 ch, cont in patt to end of row.

row 7: work 13(14:14:15) shells, 3 ch, miss next tr and ch, 1 sl.st in tr, turn.

row 8: sl.st along 3 ch, 3 ch, cont in patt to end of row but omitting 3 ch at end. 13(14:14:15) shells.

SHAPE SHOULDERS.—next row: miss first tr, (1 sl.st in ch space, 1 sl.st in each next 2 tr) 2(2:2:3) times, sl.st along 1 ch and 1 tr, work 6(7:7:7) shells, 3 ch, turn.

next row: work 6(7:7:7) shells, 3 ch, miss next tr and ch, 1 sl.st in next tr, turn.

next row: sl.st along 3 ch, (sl.st in next tr, ch, tr) 3(3:3:4) times, 3 ch, work 3(4:4:3) shells omitting 3 ch at end of last rep.

Fasten off.

Miss 5(5:7:7) centre shells. Rejoin yarn between 5/6(5/6:6/7)th shells.

row 1: 3 ch, cont in patt 17(18:18:19) times, 3 ch, turn.

row 2: work 15(16:16:17) shells, 3 ch, miss next tr and ch, 1 sl.st in next tr, turn.

row 3: sl.st along 3 ch, 3 ch, cont in patt to end of row.

row 4: work 14(15:15:16) shells, 3 ch, miss next tr and ch, 1 sl.st in next tr, turn.

row 5: sl.st along 3 ch, 3 ch, cont in patt to end of row.

row 6: work 13(14:14:15) shells, 3 ch, miss 1 tr and ch, 1 sl.st in next tr, turn.

row 7: sl.st along 3 ch, 3 ch, cont in patt to end of row.

row 8: work straight in patt.

SHAPE SHOULDER.—next row: work 10(11:11:11) shells, 3 ch, miss next tr and ch, sl.st in next tr, turn.

next row: sl.st along 3 ch, (1 sl.st in next tr, ch space, next tr) 3(3:3:4) times, 3 ch, work in patt to end of row.

next row: work 3(4:4:3) shells, 3 ch, miss next tr and ch, sl.st in next tr.

Fasten off.

BACK.—Work as for Front to **. 40(42:44:46) shells.

Rep patt row 8(9:10:11) times more.

DIVIDE FOR BACK OPENING.—next row: work 20(21:22:23) shells, 3 ch, turn.

Cont on these 20(21:22:23) shells. Rep patt

row 17 times more omitting 3 ch at end of last row.

SHAPE SHOULDER.—next row: miss 1 tr, (sl.st in 1 ch space, in each next 2 tr) 2(2:2:3) times, 1 sl.st in 1 ch space and next tr, 3 ch, work 17(18:18:18) shells, 3 ch, turn.

next row: work 13(14:14:14) shells, 3 ch, miss next tr and ch, 1 sl.st in next tr, turn.

next row: sl.st along 3 ch, (1 sl.st in next tr, ch space and tr) 3(3:3:4) times, 3 ch, work 10(11:11:10) shells.

Fasten off.

Rejoin yarn between same 2 tr as last shell at start of back opening, 3 ch, work 20(21:22:23) shells, 3 ch, turn.

next row: work 20(21:22:23) shells, 3 ch, turn. Rep patt row 16 times more.

SHAPE SHOULDER.—next row: work 17(18:18:18) shells, 3 ch, miss next tr and ch, sl.st in next tr, turn.

next row: sl.st along 3 ch, (sl.st in next tr, ch space, next tr) 3(3:3:4) times, 3 ch, cont in patt to end.

next row: work 10(11:11:10) shells, 3 ch, miss next tr and ch space, sl.st in next tr.

Fasten off.

SLEEVES.—With 2 mm (13) hook, ch 50(52:54:56) and work a foundation row as for Front. 24(25:26:27) shells.

Rep patt row 10 times ending last row with 4 ch. ***

First inc row: 1 tr in 4th ch from hook, cont in patt ending with 1 shell between last tr and turning ch, 1 tr in turning ch, 3 ch, turn.

Second inc row: 1 tr in first tr, cont in patt ending with (1 tr, 1 ch, 2 tr) in turning ch. Rep this row 4 times more.

Next inc row: 1 shell between first 2 tr, cont in patt then work 1 shell between last tr and turning ch, 3 ch, turn.

Rep pattern row 4 times more but end last row with 4 ch . ***.

Rep from *** to *** 5 times more. 36(37:38:39) shells.

Rep patt row once more omitting 3 ch at end of row.

SHAPE TOP.—row 1: as row 1 for Front Armhole Shaping but working 30(31:32:33) shells.

row 2: sl.st along 3 ch, 3 ch, work 29(30:31:32) shells, 1 tr in 3 ch space, 3 ch, turn.

row 3: miss 1 tr, work 29(30:31:32) shells, turn.

row 4: miss 1 tr, sl.st in ch space and next tr, 3 ch, work 27(28:29:30) shells, 1 tr in turning ch, 3 ch, turn.

row 5: miss 1 tr, work 27(28:29:30) shells, turn.

The feminine frill around the neck and down the front of this shirt contrasts with the formal styling of the set-in sleeves

row 6: miss 1 tr, sl.st in ch space and next tr, 3 ch, work 26(27:28:29) shells, turn.

Row 7: as row 6 but work 25(26:27:28) shells. Work 7 more rows in this way, working 1 less shell in every row.

row 15: miss 1 tr, sl.st in ch space, next 2 tr, ch space and next tr, 3 ch, work 16(17:18:19) shells, turn.

row 16: as row 15 but work 14(15:16:17) shells.

Work 2 more rows in this way, working 2 shells fewer in each row.

Work 2 more rows working 3 shells fewer in each row, ending last row with 3 ch, 1 sl.st in turning ch.

Fasten off.

BACK OPENING BORDERS.—With right side of work facing work 31 dc down left side of opening, 1 ch, turn.

next row: 1 dc, *2 ch, miss 1 dc, 1 dc in each of next 8 dc; rep from * twice more, 2 ch, miss 1 dc, 1 dc in each of last 2 dc.

next row: dc to end, working 1 dc in each 2 ch space.

Fasten off.

Work 3 rows dc along right side of opening.

FRILL.—With 2 mm (13) hook, make 3 ch.

row 1: 2 tr in 3rd ch from hook. **Do not turn.**

row 2: 3 ch, 2 tr in top of last tr of last row. **Do not turn.**—Rep 2nd row until strip is long enough to go round neck and down front twice, as shown, ending last rep with 6 ch, turn.

next row: * 1 dc in 3 ch space, (4 ch, 1 dc in same space as last dc) twice, 4 ch; rep from * to end, ending last rep with 7 ch, turn.

next row: 1 dc in first space, * 5 ch, 1 dc in next space; rep from * to end, 8 ch, turn.

next row: 1 tr in first space, * 5 ch, 1 tr in next space; rep from * to end, 8 ch, turn.

Rep last row twice more.

next row: * (1 dc, 4 ch, 1 dc) in same space, 4 ch; rep from * to last space of row, (1 dc, 4 ch, 1 sl.st) in last space.

Fasten off.

Make 2 more frills long enough to fit along each wrist edge.

LOWER EDGES.—With wrong side of Front facing, work 1 row dc along lower edge, working 1 dc in base of each shell and 1 dc in each ch space, 2 ch, turn.

row 2: 1 tr in each dc of previous row, 1 ch, turn.

row 3: 1 dc in each tr of previous row, 2 ch, turn.

Rep 2nd and 3rd rows twice more but omit 2 ch at end of last row. Fasten off.

Work back edge to match.

TO MAKE UP.—Join shoulder seams. Fold each frill into a flat spiral. Using a flat seam, sew frill round neck edge and down front. Sew a frill round each sleeve edge. Press seams. Join side and sleeve seams. Set in sleeves. Sew on buttons.

See ball band for pressing instructions.

CREW-NECK SWEATER

1953

* Easy-to-make, simply shaped crew-neck sweater with long sleeves worked in double crochet and a double knit wool yarn. Knitted ribs form the cuffs, crew neck and welts

MATERIALS.—Jaeger Prelude DK: 14(15:16:17) 50 g balls; 4.50 mm (7) crochet hook; pair of 3¾ mm (9) knitting needles.
TENSION.—9 dc to 5 cm [2 inches], 8 rows to 3 cm [1¼ inches] over stitch 1.
STITCHES.—1. double crochet; 2. k2, p2 rib.
SIZES.—To fit chest 91(97:102:107) cm [38(40:42:44) inches]. Actual measurements: 97(102:107:112) cm [40(42:44:46) inches]; length to shoulder 62(63.5:65:66) cm [24½(25:25½:26) inches]; sleeve seam 49.5 cm [19½ inches].
Figures in brackets () refer to larger sizes.
ABBREVIATIONS.—ch-chain; dc-double crochet; dec-decrease; foll-following; inc-increase; k-knit; p-purl; sl.st-slip stitch; st(s)-stitch(es); tog-together.

BACK.—With 3¾ mm (9) needles cast on 90(96:100:106) sts and work in k2, p2 rib for 11.5 cm [4½ inches] using a larger needle for last row of rib.Change to 4.50 mm (7) hook, make a ch then work 1 dc in each rib st to end of row.Work straight in dc until work measures 41 cm [16 inches].
SHAPE ARMHOLES.—Sl.st across 8 sts, work to last 8 sts, turn. ** Work straight until armholes measure 21.5(23:23:24) cm [8½(9:9:9½) inches].
SHAPE SHOULDERS.—Sl.st across 10(11:12:13) sts, dec2 tog, work to end. Repeat this row.Sl.st across 11(12:13:14) sts, dec 2tog, work to end. Repeat this row.
Fasten off.

FRONT.—Work as for Back to **
Work straight until armhole measures 13 cm [5 inches].
SHAPE NECK.—Work 28(30:31:33) sts, turn.
next row: dec 2tog at neck edge, work to armhole edge.
next row: work to last 2 sts at neck edge, dec 2tog.
Continue dec in this way until there are 23(25:27:29) sts. Then work straight until armhole measures same as for Back.
SHAPE SHOULDERS.—Work as for Back. Rejoin yarn to other side of work leaving 18(20:22:24) sts at centre and work the remaining 28(30:31:33) sts as for first side.
Fasten off.

SLEEVES.—With 3¾ mm (9) needles cast on 44(48:48:52) sts and work in k2, p2 rib for 7.5 cm [3 inches]. Using a larger size needle, inc 1 st either end of last row. Change to 4.50 mm (7) hook and work 1 dc st in each rib st to end of row. Cont in dc increasing 1 st either side of

next and every foll 10th row until there are 56(60:64:66) sts. Work straight until sleeve measures 49.5 cm [19½ inches].
SHAPE TOP.—Sl.st across 8 sts, work to end; sl.st across 8 sts work to end. Work straight for 13 cm [5 inches] then dec 1 st at both ends of next and every alternate row until armhole measures 18 cm [7 inches]. Fasten off.

NECKBAND.—Join right shoulder seam. With 3¾ mm (9) needles, pick up and k approximately 100(104:104:108) sts round neck. Work in k2, p2 rib for 2.5 cm [1 inch]. Cast off loosely ribwise.

TO MAKE UP.—Set sleeves into place and sew. Sew sleeve and side seams.
See ball band for pressing instructions.

TWO PIECE DRESS

1964

** *This easy-fitting two piece dress with shirt collared pullover top and slender skirt is crocheted in a combination of half trebles alternating with open work bands of trebles*

MATERIALS.—Sirdar Classical Double Crepe: 22(24:26:28:30) 50 g balls; 4.50 mm (7) crochet hook; 25 cm [10 inch] zip fastener; elastic for waist; hooks and eyes.

TENSION.—13 sts and 9 rows to 7.5 cm [3 inches] over stitch pattern.

STITCHES.—1. half trebles; 2. trebles.

SIZES.—To fit bust 81(86:92:97:102) cm [32(34:36:38:40) inches]; to fit hip 86(92:97: 102:107) cm [34(36:38:40:42) inches]. Actual measurements: bust 88(95:99:104:109) cm [34½(37¼:39:41:43) inches]; hip 92.5(97.5:102: 106.5:111) cm [36½(38¼:40:42:43¾) inches]; length of top 59(60.5:61:61.5:62) cm [23¼(23¾: 24:24¼:24½) inches]; sleeve seam 42 cm [16½ inches]; length of skirt 68.5 cm [27 inches]. Figures in brackets () refer to larger sizes.

ABBREVIATIONS.—alt-alternate; beg-beginning; ch-chain; cont-continue; dec-decrease; foll-following; htr-half treble; inc-increase; rem-remaining; rep-repeat; sl.st-slip stitch; st(s)-stitch(es); tr-treble; yrh-yarn round hook.

TOP BACK.—With 4.50 mm (7) hook, make a loose ch of 76(80:84:88:92), yrh, put hook into 3rd ch from hook and work 1 htr in this and each ch to end of work, 2 turning ch. (75:81:85:89:93 sts).

NOTE: always count the turning ch as first st on following row.

row 1: 1 htr in each st to end, 2 turning ch.

rows 2-3: as row 1.

row 4: 1 tr in first st. * miss 1 st, 2 tr in next st; rep from * to end, 2 turning ch.

row 5: Work 2 tr in space between each 2 tr group to end, 1 tr in turning ch, 2 turning ch.

row 6: 1 tr between 1st and 2nd tr, * 2 tr in space between each 2 tr group; rep from * ending with 2 tr in turning ch, 2 turning ch.

row 7: 1 htr in first st, 1 htr in every stitch to end, 2 turning ch.

(Count sts to make sure you have the same number as you started with.)

These 7 rows form pattern.

Work in pattern for 49 rows or desired length to underarm omitting 2 ch at end of last row. **

SHAPE ARMHOLES.— sl.st over 4(4:5:5:6) sts, 2 ch, work to last 3(3:4:4:5) sts, turn.

Dec 1 st at each end of every alt row until 61(63:65:67:69) sts remain. Work until arm-

holes are 17(18.5:19:19.5:20) cm [6¾(7¼:7½: 7¾:8¼) inches] measured on the straight.
SHAPE SHOULDERS.—Sl.st over 10(11: 11:11:11) sts, 2 ch, work to last 9(10:10:10:10) sts, turn. Sl.st over 10(10:10:9:9) sts, 2 ch, work to last 9(9:9:10:10) sts.
Fasten off leaving 25(25:27:27:29) sts in centre for neck.

TOP FRONT.—Work as for Back to **.
SHAPE ARMHOLES AND DIVIDE FOR FRONT OPENING.— sl.st over 4(4:5:5:6) sts, 2 ch, work across next 30(32:33:35:36) sts, turn.
Finish this side first.
*** Dec 1 st at armhole every alt row until 26(27:28:29:30) sts remain. Work until armhole measures same as Back, ending with same patt row as armhole edge.
SHAPE SHOULDERS.—row 1: sl.st over 10(11:11:11:12) sts, 2 ch, work to end, 2 turning ch.
row 2: work 8(8:9:9:10) sts for neck.
Fasten off.
Count 7 sts across centre, join yarn to next st, 2 ch, work to last 3(3:4:4:5) sts, turn.
Now work from *** to match first side.

COLLAR.—Sew shoulder seams. Join yarn to right front at neck edge.
Work in rows of htr.
row 1: work across right front, back of neck and across left front, 2 turning ch. (41:41:45:45:49) sts
Work 1 row.
row 3: work 2(2:3:3:4) sts, * work 2 htr in next st (called inc 1), work 4; rep from * ending last rep 2(2:3:3:4) htr. (8 sts increased)
Work 3 more rows.
row 7: work 2(2:3:3:4) sts, * inc 1, work 5; rep from * ending last rep 3(3:4:4:5) htr, 2 turning ch.
Work 1 row.
Break yarn and join to lower edge of front opening at right side.
row 1: work htrs up front edge to corner of collar, work 3 htr into corner, work across collar, 3 htr into corner, work to lower edge of left side of opening, 1 turning ch.
Rep last row twice more, then work 1 row of sl.st.
Fasten off.

SLEEVES.—With 4.50 mm (7) hook work 38(40:42:44:46) ch. Work in pattern having 37(39:41:43:45) sts.
Work 10 rows inc 1 st at each end of next and every foll 5th row until there are 49(51:55:57:61) sts. Work to end of 49th row

as for Back or until desired length.
SHAPE TOP.—row 1: sl.st over 4(4:5:5:6) sts, 2 ch, work to last 3(3:4:4:5) sts, 2 turning ch.
Dec 1 st at each end of next 9(10:11:12:13) rows. (24 sts).
next row: sl.st over 4 sts, 2 ch, work to last 3 sts, turn.
Rep last row once more.
Fasten off.

TO MAKE UP TOP.—Set in sleeves. Sew side and sleeve seams. Sew vent edges. Work 1 row of sl.st around lower edge and sleeve.
See ball band for pressing instructions.

SKIRT BACK.—Beg at waist, with 4.50 mm (7) hook make a loose ch of 52(56:60:64:68) sts, turn. Work in patt having 51(55:59:63:67) sts. Work 3 rows.
row 4: 2 htr in first st, work 12(13:14:15:16) sts, 2 htr in next st (called inc 1), work 22(24:26:28:30) sts, inc 1, work to last st, inc 1. Work 3 rows
row 8: work (14:15:16:17:18) sts, inc 1, work 24(26:28:30:32) sts, inc 1, work to end.
Work 2 rows.
row 11: inc 1, work 13(14:15:16:17) sts, inc 1, work 26(28:30:32:34) sts, inc 1, work to last st, inc 1.
Work 3 rows.
row 15: work 15(16:17:18:19) sts, inc 1, work 28(30:32:34:36) sts, inc 1, work to end.
Work 2 rows.
row 18: inc 1, work 14(15:16:17:18) sts, inc 1, work 30(32:34:36:38) sts, inc 1, work to last st, inc 1.
Work 3 rows.
row 22: work 16(17:18:19:20) sts, inc 1, work 32(34:36:38:40) sts, inc 1, work to end.
Work 2 rows.
row 25: inc 1, work 15(16:17:18:19) sts, inc 1, work 34(36:38:40:42) sts, inc 1, work to last st, inc 1. (73:77:81:85:89) htr.
Now inc 1 at each end of every foll 7th row until there are 79(83:87:91:95) sts.
Work until skirt measures 69 cm [27 inches] or desired length.
Fasten off.

SKIRT FRONT.—Work as for Back.

TO MAKE UP SKIRT.—Sew side seams leaving 20 cm [8 inch] opening at top of left side. Set in zip fastener. Cut elastic to required size. Sew hooks and eyes to each end. Sew elastic to inside of waist. Work 1 row of sl.st around lower edge.
See ball band for pressing instructions.

LACY PATTERNED SWEATER

1979

** *Lightweight, loose-fitting jumper with short sleeves worked in a lacy shell pattern. Double crochet edges the deep boat neckline and knitted ribs form the cuffs and welts*

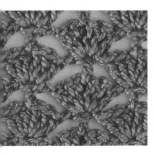

MATERIALS.—Emu Perle: 9(10) 50 g balls; 3 mm (3) crochet hook; pair of 3 mm (11) knitting needles.

TENSION.—2 pattern repeats to 7 cm [2¾ inches]; 2 rows to 4 cm [approx 1½ inches] over stitch 1.

STITCHES.—1. shell pattern; 2. k2, p2 rib.

SIZES.—To fit bust 86-91(97-102) cm [34-36(38-40) inches]. Actual measurement 101(110) cm [39¾(43¼) inches]; length to shoulder 54(56) cm [21¼(22) inches]; sleeve seam 20 cm [8 inches].

Figures in brackets () refer to larger sizes.

ABBREVIATIONS.—beg-beginning; ch-chain; cont-continue; dc-double crochet; k-knit; p-purl; patt-pattern; rep-repeat; st(s)-stitch(es); tr-treble; yrh-yarn round hook.

BACK.—With 3 mm (3) hook make 107(110) ch, yrh, hook in 3rd ch from hook and work 1 dc in this and all subsequent ch from hook to end, 2 turning ch. This is the foundation row.

next row: dc in every dc worked in previous row, 3 turning ch.

row 1: miss 3 dc, 6 tr in 4th dc, 1 ch, miss 3 dc, * 1 tr in 4th dc, 1 ch, 6 tr in 4th ch, 1 ch; rep from * to last 8 dc, 6 tr, 1 ch, miss 3 ch, 1 ch, 1 tr, 1 ch, miss 3 ch, 3 tr in last st, 3 turning ch.

row 2: * 6 tr in top of 1 tr of previous row, 1 ch, miss 3 ch, 1 tr in between 3rd and 4th tr of shell, 1 ch; rep from * to end.

Cont these two patt rows until work measures 42(44) cm [16½(17¼) inches]. Mark 15 cm [6 inches] in from each side edge.

SHAPE NECK.—Work in patt to first marker, turn and patt to end. Fasten off.

With right side facing, join yarn to other side of neck and work to other marker.

Fasten off.

FRONT.—Work as given for Back until Front measures 36(38) cm [14¼(15) inches].

SHAPE NECK.—Work as for Back until Front measures 42(44) cm [16½:17¼) inches]. Fasten off.

Work other side to match.

WELTS.—(work 2) With right side facing, join yarn to lower edge, with 3 mm (11) needle, pick up and k 134(142) sts.

row 1: p2, * k2, p2; rep from * to end.

row 2: k2, * p2, k2; rep from * to end.

Rep these 2 rows for 8 cm [3¼ inches], ending with row 1.

Cast off in rib.

Ribbed cuffs neatly finish the lacy shell pattern sleeves

SLEEVES.—With 3 mm (3) hook make 79 ch, yrh, hook into 3rd ch from hook and work 1 dc in this and all subsequent ch to end of row, 3 turning ch. This forms the foundation row.

row 1: 5 tr in first dc, * miss 3 dc, 1 ch, 1 tr in 4th dc, miss 3 dc, 1 ch, 6 tr in 4th dc; rep from * to last 6 tr, miss 3 dc, 1 ch, 1 tr in last dc, 3 turning ch.

row 2: 2 tr in ch space, 1ch, 1 tr in top of 6 tr worked on previous row, 1 ch, 6 tr in top of 1 tr; rep from * ending with 3 tr in last group tr worked on previous row, 3 turning ch.

row 3: 6 tr in top of 1 tr of previous row, 1 ch, 1 tr in top of 6 tr of previous row, work in patt ending with 1 tr in top of 3rd tr, 3 turning ch.

row 4: 5 tr in ch space, 1 ch, 1 tr in top of 6 tr, work in patt to end, 6 tr in top of last tr, 3 turning ch.

row 5: 2 tr, 1 ch, * 1 tr, 1 ch, 6 tr, 1 ch; rep from * ending with 3 tr in last st, 3 turning ch.

row 6: 1 ch, 6 tr, * 1 ch, 1 tr, 1 ch, 6 tr; rep from * ending with 1 tr in last st, 3 turning ch.

row 7: 5 tr, * 1 ch, 1 tr, 1 ch, 6 tr; rep from * ending with 6 tr in last st, 3 turning ch.

row 8: 1 ch, * 1 tr, 1 ch, 6 tr, 1 ch; rep from * ending with 1 tr in last st, 3 turning ch.

row 9: 1 ch, * 6 tr, 1 ch, 1 tr, 1 ch; rep from * ending with 1 tr in last st, 3 turning ch.

row 10: 2 tr in ch space, * 1 ch, 1 tr, 1 ch, 6 tr; rep from * ending with 6 tr in last st, 3 turning ch.

row 11: 2 tr in ch space, * 1 ch, 1 tr, 1 ch, 6 tr; rep from * ending with 1 tr in last st, 3 turning ch.

row 12: 5 tr, * 1 ch, 1 tr, 1 ch, 6 tr; rep from * ending with 1 tr in last st, 3 turning ch.

row 13: 2 tr in ch space, * 1 ch, 1 tr, 1 ch, 6 tr; rep from * ending with 3 tr in last st, 3 turning ch.

rows 14 & 15: work 2 rows straight in patt. Fasten off.

CUFFS.—With right side facing, join in yarn and using a 3 mm (11) needle, pick up and k 82 sts evenly along lower edge of sleeve. Work 2.5 cm [1 inch] in rib as given for welts. Cast off in rib.

NECK EDGING.-Join shoulder seams. With right side facing and beg at centre back neck, work 2 rows of dc all round neck edge. Fasten off.

TO MAKE UP.—Fold sleeves in half lengthwise, with centres to shoulder seams, sew in place. Sew side and sleeve seams. See ball band for pressing instructions.

SIMPLE CARDIGAN JACKET

1 9 4 9

* A simple, stylish V-necked cardigan jacket is worked in double crochet. The front bands are worked on to the main parts for pattern contrast. Crab stitch edges the sleeves

MATERIALS.—Patons Diploma 4 ply: 12(13:15:16) 50 g balls; 3 mm (10) and 3.50 mm (9) crochet hooks; 6 buttons.
TENSION.—12 sts to 5 cm [2 inches] over pattern using 3.50 mm (9) hook.
STITCHES.—1. double crochet worked in front loop only (NOTE: It helps when making up if the first and last st are worked through **both** double crochet loops); 2. crab stitch.
SIZES.—To fit chest 96 (102:106:111) cm [38(40:42:44) inches]. Actual measurements 102(106:111:117) cm [40(42:44:46) inches]; length 67(67:68.5:68.5) cm [26½(26½:27:27) inches]; sleeve seam 48 cm [19 inches].
Figures in brackets () refer to larger sizes.

ABBREVIATONS.—ch-chain; dc-double crochet; dec-decrease; inc-increase; sl.st-slip stitch; yrh-yarn round hook.

BACK.—With 3.50 mm (9) hook make 121(127:133:139) ch, yrh, put hook in 2nd ch from hook and work 1 dc in this and all subsequent ch to end of row, 1 turning ch. 120(126:132:138) sts.
next row: 1 dc in first st, 1 dc in front loop only of every st to last st, 1 dc in last st, 1 turning ch.
This row forms pattern.
Continue in pattern and work straight until work measures 46 cm [18 inches].
SHAPE ARMHOLES.—Sl.st across 10 sts, work to last 10 sts, turn.
Continue straight until armhole measures 21.5(21.5:23:23) cm [8½(8½:9:9) inches]. On last row work to last 30 sts, turn.
next row: work next 40(46:52:58) sts.
Fasten off.

LEFT FRONT.—With 3.50 mm (9) hook, make 68(71:74:77) ch, yrh, hook into second ch from hook and work 1 dc in this and all subsequent ch to end of row, 1 turning ch. 67(70:73:76) sts.
Continue in pattern and work straight until work measures 46 cm [18 inches] ending at armhole edge.
SHAPE ARMHOLE AND NECK.—Sl.st across 10 sts at armhole edge, work to end. Keeping armhole edge straight, dec 1 st at neck edge on next 2 rows, then 1 row straight. Continue dec in this way until there are 30 sts. Work straight until work measures same as Back.
Fasten off.

RIGHT FRONT.—Work as for Left Front reversing all shapings.

SLEEVES.—With 3.50 mm (9) hook make 57(61:65:69) ch, yrh, hook into second ch

from hook and work 1 dc in this and all subsequent ch to end of row, 1 turning ch 56(60:64:68) sts.

Continue in pattern inc 1 st at either edge of first row and then every 6th row until there are 88(92:96:100) sts. Continue straight until work measures 48 cm [19 inches].

SHAPE TOP.—next row: work to last 10 sts, turn.

Work next row to last 10 sts, turn.

Dec 1 st each end of next 2 rows, then 1 row straight. Continue dec in this way until there are 24(30:34:38) sts.

Fasten off.

With 3 mm (10) hook work crab st edging around cuff thus.

row 1: work in dc round cuff. Do not turn work.

row 2: work in dc round cuff.

Fasten off.

BORDERS.—Sew shoulder and side seams. With 3.50 mm (9) hook and right side of work facing, work 1 dc in every row along front edge, in every st along back and in every row down second front edge, 1 turning ch. Continuing in dc, work 2 more rows.

MAKE BUTTONHOLES.—row 4: work 4 dc, * ch 4, miss 4 sts, work 15 sts; repeat from * until 6 buttonholes have been made.

row 5: work in dc working 1 dc in each ch st.

rows 6-8: work in dc.

Change to 3 mm (10) hook and work in crab stitch around band and hem.

TO MAKE UP.—Sew sleeve seams, sew sleeves into armholes. Sew on buttons. See ball band for pressing instructions.

TWEED JACKET

1954

* Simple double crochet and a fine wool tweed yarn make a comfortable cardigan jacket with separately worked front bands and knitted ribs to make the cuffs and the neat neck edging

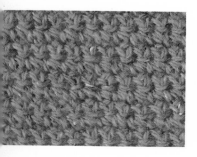

MATERIALS.—Rowan Fine Tweed: 22(24:26:28) 25 g hanks; 2.50 mm (2) crochet hook; pair of 3 mm (11) knitting needles; 8 buttons.

TENSION.—6 sts and 7 rows to 2.5 cm [1 inch] over double crochet.

STITCHES.—1. double crochet; 2. k1, p1 rib.

SIZES.—To fit bust 86(91:97:102) cm [34(36:38:40) inches]. Actual measurement 97(102:107:112) cm [38(40:42:44) inches]; length from shoulder 62(63.5:63.5:65) cm [24½(25:25:25½) inches]; sleeve seam 49.5 cm [19½ inches].

Figures in brackets () refer to larger sizes

ABBREVIATIONS.—alt-alternate; ch-chain; cont-continue; dec-decrease; inc-increase; k-knit; rem-remaining; rep-repeat; p-purl; sl.st-slip stitch; st(s)-stitch(es); yrh-yarn round hook.

BACK.—With 2.50 mm (2) hook, make 115(121:127:133) ch, yrh, hook into 2nd ch from hook and work 1 dc in this and all subsequent ch to end of row, 1 turning ch. 114(120:126:132) sts.

Work straight in dc until work measures 40.5 cm [16 inches].

SHAPE ARMHOLE.—Sl.st across 2 sts, work to last 2 sts, turn.

next row: sl.st across 2 sts, work to last 2 sts, turn.

next row: dec 2tog at each edge on this and every alt row until there are 94(98:102:106) sts.

Work straight until armhole measures 21.5(23:23:24) cm [8½(9:9:9½) inches].

SHAPE SHOULDER.—Sl.st across 3 sts, work to last 3 sts, turn. Rep this row until 46(50:54:58) sts remain.

next row: sl.st across 5(6:7:8) sts, work to last 5(6:7:8) sts. 36(38:40:42) sts remain.

Fasten off.

LEFT FRONT.—With 2.50 mm (2) hook make 55(58:61:64) ch, hook into 2nd ch from hook and work 1 dc in this and all subsequent ch to end of row, 1 turning ch. 54(57:60:63) sts.

Work straight until work measures 40.5 cm [16 inches] ending at armhole edge.

SHAPE ARMHOLE.—Sl.st across 2 sts, work to end.

Work to last 2 sts, turn.

next row: dec 1 st at armhole edge on this and every alt row until 42(44:46:48) sts remain.

Cont straight until armhole measures 15(16.5:16.5:18) cm [6(6½:6½:7) inches].

SHAPE NECK.—Dec 2tog at neck edge on every row until 29(30:31:32) sts remain. Work straight until armhole measures same as for Back ending at armhole edge.
SHAPE SHOULDER.—Sl.st across 3 sts, work to end.
next row: work to last 3 sts, turn.
Rep these two rows three more times.
next row: sl.st across last 5(6:7:8) sts.

RIGHT FRONT.—Work as for Left Front reversing all shapings.

SLEEVES.—With 3 mm (11) needles, cast on 56 sts and work in k1, p1 rib for 9 cm [3½ inches] using a larger needle for last row. Change to 2.50 mm (2) hook, 1 ch, work 1 dc in every st of rib.
Work 1 row.
next row: inc 1 st at each end of row.
Work 3 rows.
next and every 4th row: inc 1 dc at each end of row until there are 78(82:86:90) sts.
Work straight until work measures 49.5 cm [19½ inches].
SHAPE TOP.—Sl.st across 2 sts, work to last 2 sts, turn. 74(78:82:86) sts.
Dec 1 st at either end of every alt row until 34(38:42:46) sts rem then 2 sts either end of every row until 14 sts rem.
Fasten off.

FRONT BANDS.—Work a line of dc down left front, approx 143(149:149:155) dc. Work 10 rows. Mark position for buttons.
Fasten off.
Work the same number of dc down right front. Work 4 rows.
MAKE BUTTONHOLES.—Work 3 sts, sl.st across 4 sts. Cont in dc making buttonholes to correspond with positions marked on Button band.
next row: work 1 row in dc working 4 ch over sl.sts.
Work 4 more rows working 1 dc in each ch in the first row. Fasten off.

COLLAR BAND.—Sew shoulder seams. With 3 mm (11) needles pick up and k approximately 116(120:120:124) sts starting at beg of left front band, up side neck, across back, down side neck to end of right front band. Work in k1, p1 rib for 4 cm [1½ inches].
Cast off.

TO MAKE UP.—Sew side and sleeve seams. Set in sleeves. Work sl.st down front bands and round edge of garment.
See ball band for pressing instructions.

43

JUMPER WITH BOW

1932

** *The stripe on this design was adapted from the original to an elegant single stripe and matching bow trim. The body is worked in a shell pattern with knitted cuffs and welts*

MATERIALS.—Emu Superwash 4 ply: 8(10) 50 g balls Main colour; 2(2) 50 g balls Contrast colour; 4 mm (8) crochet hook; pair of 2¾ mm (12) knitting needles.
TENSION.—One 5 tr group and dc to 2.5 cm [1 inch]; 4 rows to 3 cm [approx 1¼ inches].
STITCHES.—1. shell pattern; 2. k1, p1 rib.
SIZES.—To fit bust 81-86(91-97) cm [32-34(36-38) inches]. Actual measurement 95(105) cm [37½(41¼) inches]; length 58.5 cm [23 inches]; sleeve seam 43 cm [17 inches]. Figures in brackets () refer to larger sizes.
ABBREVIATIONS.—C-contrast; ch-chain; cont-continue; dc-double crochet; dtr-double treble; inc-increase; k-knit; M-main; p-purl; patt-pattern; rep-repeat; sl.st-slip stitch; st(s)-stitch(es); tr-treble.

BACK.—With M and 4 mm (8) hook make 118(130) ch loosely and work 2 tr in 4th ch from hook, * miss 2 ch, 1 dc in next ch, miss 2 ch, 5 tr in next ch; rep from * to last 6 ch, miss 2 ch, 1 dc in next ch, miss 2 ch, 3 tr in last ch. This is the foundation row.
row 1: (wrong side) 1 ch, 1 dc in first tr, * 2 ch, 1 tr in dc, 2 ch, 1 dc in centre of 5 tr; rep from * to end, working last dc in top of 3 ch.
row 2: 1 ch, 1 dc in dc, * 5 tr in tr, 1 dc in dc; rep from * to end. (19 5 tr groups).
row 3: 5 ch, 1 dc in centre of 5 tr, 2 ch, 1 tr in dc, * 2 ch, 1 dc in centre of 5 tr, 2 ch, 1 tr in dc; rep from * to end.
row 4: 3 ch, 2 tr in tr, 1 dc in dc, * 5 tr in tr, 1 dc in dc; rep from * ending with 3 tr in turning ch.
These four rows form pattern.
Rep these 4 rows nine times more then work row 1 again. **
Change to C and work row 2. Cont with C.
SHAPE ARMHOLES.—next row: sl.st to centre of 5 tr, 1 ch, 1 dc in tr, patt to end working last dc in centre of 5 tr, turn.
next row: as row 2 of patt. Rep last 2 rows 3 times. *** Work 1st of these rows again. Change to M.
next row: as row 2 of patt. [14(16) 5 tr groups] Patt 15(17) rows, ending with row 1 of patt. Fasten off.

WELT.—With right side facing, using 2¾ mm (12) needles and M, pick up and k 116(128) sts along remaining edge of foundation row.
row 1: p7(9), (p1, k1, p1) in next st, p9; rep from * ending last rep p8. [138:152 sts].
Work 26 rows in k1, p1 rib. Cast off ribwise.

FRONT.—Work as for Back to **. Change to C.
SHAPE BOW.—next row: 1 ch, 1 dc in dc, (5 tr in tr, 1 dc in dc) 9(10) times, take a separate length of C and join to same dc as last dc was worked and make 137 ch loosely, miss 2 ch, 1 tr and 2 ch at centre front and join ch to next dc then over this length of ch, work * miss 2

ch, 5 tr in next ch, miss 2 ch, 1 dc in next ch; rep from * 21 times, miss 2 ch, 5 tr in next ch, miss last 2 ch, 1 dc in same dc as ch is joined, (5 tr in tr, 1 dc in dc) 9(10) times.

SHAPE ARMHOLES.—Work as for Back to *** [37(39) 5 tr groups].

Work 1st armhole shaping row again. Change to M.

SHAPE NECK.—row 1: 1 ch, 1 dc in dc, * 5 tr in tr, 1 dc in dc; rep from * 5(6) times, 3 tr in next tr, turn.

Continue on these sts only.

row 2: 1 ch, 1 dc in first tr, * 2 ch, 1 tr in dc, 2 ch, 1 dc in centre of 5 tr; rep from * to end.

row 3: 3 ch, 2 tr in dc, 1 dc in dc, * 5 tr in tr, 1 dc in dc; rep from * to end.

row 4: sl.st to centre of 5 tr, 1 ch, 1 dc in tr, patt as set to end.

Rep rows 4 & 5 five times. Patt 3(5) rows with sts as set.

Fasten off.

With right side facing, rejoin M to 7th (9th) tr from left side of work.

row 1: 3 ch, 2 tr in tr, * 1 dc in dc, 5 tr in tr; rep from * 5(6) times more, 1 dc in dc.

row 2: 5 ch, * 1 dc in centre of 5 tr, 2 ch, 1 tr in dc, 2 ch; rep from * ending 1 dc in 3rd ch.

row 3: 1 ch, 1 dc in dc, * 5 tr in tr, 1 dc in dc; rep from * ending 3 tr in 3rd ch.

row 4: 1 ch, 1 dc in first tr, * 2 ch, 1 tr in dc 2 ch, 1 dc in centre of 5 tr; rep from * to end.

row 5: 1 ch, 1 dc in dc, * 5 tr in tr, 1 dc in dc; rep from * to end.

Rep rows 4 & 5 five times, then patt 3(5) rows with sts as set.

Fasten off.

WELT.—Work as given for Back.

SLEEVES.—With 4 mm (8) hook and M make 64(70) ch loosely. Work foundation row as given for Back. Rep 1st to 4th pattern rows of Back twice then 1st and 2nd rows again. [10 5 tr groups].

1st inc row: (wrong side) 6 ch, 1 tr in 1st dc, * 2 ch, 1 dc in centre of 5 tr, 2 ch, 1 tr in dc; rep from * ending with 2 ch, 1 tr, 1 dtr in same dc as last tr.

2nd inc row: 1 ch, 1 dc in dtr, 5 tr in tr, patt to last 5 ch, 1 dc in 3rd ch.

Patt 8 rows straight, then rep 2 inc rows. Rep last 10 rows twice. Patt 7 rows. Change to C. next row: as 2nd patt row. [14(15) 5 tr groups].

SHAPE TOP.—Work as given for armhole shaping of Back to ***.

Work 1st row again. Change to M.

Work 2nd armhole shaping row, then 1st and 2nd armhole shaping rows 4 times. [5(6) 5 tr groups].

Work 1st armhole shaping row again.

Fasten off.

CUFFS.—With right side facing, using $2\frac{3}{4}$ mm (12) needles and M, pick up and k 62(68) sts along remaining edge of foundation ch. P 1 row. Work 16 rows in k1, p1 rib.

Cast off ribwise.

TO MAKE UP.—Carefully matching pattern, join both shoulder seams. Set in sleeves matching contrast band. With M, work an edging of 32 dc along sides of front neck and 28 dc along back neck. Join side and sleeve seams.

BOW.—With C and 4 mm (8) hook make 7 ch loosely.

row 1: 1 dc in 2nd ch, 1 dc in each ch to end.

next row: 1 ch, miss 1 dc, 1 dc in each next 5 dc, 1 dc in turning ch.

Rep row 2 18 times.

Fasten off.

Fold inner ends of bow extension outwards and making sure patt of main part lies flat, catch stitch these folded edges together. Place remainder of extension over this, join and secure at centre, gathering work. Wrap knot around centre and join ends on wrong side. See ball band for pressing instructions.

SWEATER WITH POCKETS

1964

* This crew-neck, long sleeved sweater with two neat pockets is worked in a lightly textured pattern. Double crochet is used to edge the sleeves, neckband and hems

MATERIALS.—Pingouin France: 14(15:16: 17:18:19) 50 g balls; 4 mm (8) crochet hook; 4.50 (7) crochet hook.

TENSION.—24 sts and 28 rows to 10 cm [4 inches] over pattern.

STITCHES.—1. textured pattern; 2. double crochet.

SIZES.—To fit chest 86(91:97:102:107:112) cm [34(36:38:40:42:44) inches]. Actual measurement 91(97:102:107:112:117) cm [36(38: 40:42:44:46) inches]; length 65(67:69:70:71.5: 72.5) cm [25½(26½:27¼:27¾:28¼:28¾) inches]; sleeve seam 46 cm [18 inches].

Figures in brackets () relate to larger sizes.

ABBREVIATIONS.—Alt-alternate; beg-beginning; ch-chain; cont-continue; dc-double crochet; dec-decrease; foll-following; inc-increase; rem-remaining; rep-repeat; sl.st-slip stitch; st(s)-stitch(es); tr-treble.

BACK.—With 4.50 mm (7) hook make 100(106:112:118:124:130) ch, hook into first ch from hook and work 1 dc in this and all subsequent ch to end of row. Work in dc for 8 rows, inc 11 sts evenly across row.

next row: 2 ch [counts as 1 dc], * (1 dc, 1 ch, 1 tr) in next st, miss 2 sts; rep from * ending with 1 dc in last st, 1 turning ch. This is the foundation row.

row 1: miss first dc and next tr. * (1 dc, 1 ch, 1 tr) in next ch space, miss 1 dc and 1 tr; rep from * ending with (1 dc, 1 ch, 1 tr) in last ch space, miss next dc, 1 dc in top of turning ch. Row 1 forms pattern.

Cont in patt until work measures 43 cm [17 inches] ending with right side facing.

SHAPE RAGLAN.—Sl.st across first 3 sts, work in patt to last 3 sts, turn, 1 ch, cont in patt dec 1 st at each end of next 0(0:0:2:2:4) rows then at each end of every alt row until 43(44:45:44:45:44) sts rem.

Work 2 rows in patt then fasten off. When working raglans work patt as far as possible, then finish with dc to complete row.

POCKET LININGS.—With 4.50 mm (7) hook, make 33 ch and work in patt for 9 cm [3½ inches].

Fasten off.

FRONT.—Work as for Back until work measures 15 cm [6 inches] ending with right side facing.

INSERT POCKETS.—Pattern 11(12:14: 16:18:20) sts, sl.st across next 32 sts, patt 24(27:30:32:34:36) sts, sl.st across next 32 sts, patt to end.

next row: work in patt working pocket lining sts across sl.sts keeping patt correct. Cont in pattern until there are 63(64:65:64:65) sts ending with right side facing.

SHAPE NECK.—Keeping raglan dec correct, work 22 sts and turn. Work on these sts for first side, dec 1 st at neck edge on next and foll 3rd row, then on every alt row 9 times. Cont with raglan dec until 3 sts rem. (Should be the same length as Back raglan; if not, work any additional rows needed.)
Fasten off.

Sl.st across centre 19(20:21:20:21:20) sts, work 2nd side to match first side.

SLEEVES.—With 4.50 mm (7) hook, make 46(46:46:50:50:50) ch, hook into 2nd ch from hook and work 1 dc in this and all subsequent ch to end of row. Work 8 rows in dc, inc 1 st at each end of last row.

Now work in patt as on body at the same time and keeping patt correct, inc 1 st at each end of every foll 4th row until there are 98(98:98:104:104:104) sts. Cont in patt until work measures 46 cm [18 inches] ending with right side facing.

SHAPE RAGLAN.—Sl.st across first 3 sts, patt to last 3 sts, 1 turning ch. Now keeping patt correct, dec 1 st at each end of next and every foll 3rd row 3(10:10:8:8:10:10) times, then at each end of every alt row until 18(18:18:18:18:18) sts rem, work any rows needed to bring raglan to same depth as Back.
Fasten off.

NECKBAND.—Join front and right back raglan sleams. With 4.50 mm (7) hook and right side facing, starting at left sleeve, work in dc evenly around neck edge for 3 rows. Change to 4 mm (8) hook and work a further 3 rows in dc.
Fasten off.

TO MAKE UP.—Join left back raglan and neck seams. Sew side and sleeve seams. See ball band for pressing instructions.

FRINGED JUMPER

1961

* A simple dropped stitch adds texture to this easy-fitting, round necked jumper with elbow length sleeves worked in double knit wool. Soft fringes edge the hem and sleeves

MATERIALS.—Emu Superwash DK: 12 (13:14) 50 g balls; 4 mm (8) crochet hook.
TENSION.—18 sts and 12 rows to 10 cm [4 inches] over pattern.
STITCHES.—1. trebles; 2. double crochet.
SIZES.—To fit bust 86(91:97) cm [34(36:38) inches]. Actual measurements 99(105:111) cm [39(41¼:43¾) inches]; length from shoulder excluding fringe 55(57:59) cm [21¾(22½:23¼) inches]; sleeve seam excluding fringe 23 cm [9 inches].

Figures in brackets () refer to larger sizes.
ABBREVIATIONS.—alt-alternate; beg-beginning; ch-chain; cont-continue; dc-double crochet; dec-decrease; foll-following; inc-increase; patt-pattern; rem-remaining; rep-repeat; sl.st-slip stitch; st(s)-stitch(es); tr-treble; yrh-yarn round hook.

BACK.—With 4 mm (8) hook, make 92(98:104) ch, yrh, hook in 5th ch from hook, 1 ch, miss 1 ch, * 1 tr in each next 5 sts, 1 ch, miss 1 ch; rep from * ending with 1 tr in each last 2 ch, 3 turning ch. 89:95:101 sts.
This is the foundation row.
row 1: miss first st, 1 tr in next st, * 1 tr in foundation ch drawing a long loop through so as not to pucker work, 1 tr in each next 2 sts, 1 ch, miss 1 tr, 1 tr in each next 2 sts; rep from * to end, 3 turning ch.
row 2: miss first st, 1 tr in next tr, 1 ch, miss 1 tr, * 1 tr in each next 2 sts, 1 tr in tr 2 rows below drawing a long loop through, 1 tr in each next 2 sts, 1 ch, miss 1 tr, 1 tr in each next 2 sts; rep from * to end, 3 turning ch.
row 3: miss first st, 1 tr in next st, * 1 tr in tr 2 rows below drawing a long loop through, 1 tr in each next 2 sts, 1 ch, miss 1 tr, 1 tr in each next 2 sts; rep from * to end, 3 turning ch.
Rows 2 & 3 form patt.
NOTE: Pattern is reversible but for convenience the 2nd row will be considered to be the right side.
Cont in patt until Back measures 34 cm [13¼ inches] ending with a wrong side row.
SHAPE ARMHOLES.—next row: sl.st over 3 sts, patt to last 3 sts, turn.
Note: When shaping, work 1 tr in place of (1 ch, miss 1tr).
Dec 1 st at each end of next 6(7:8) rows.
Work straight on rem 71(75:79) sts until armhole measures 19(21:23) cm [7½(8¼:9) inches] ending with a wrong side row.
SHAPE NECK.—row 1: patt 25(26:27) sts, turn.

Self-colour fringing provides an unusual trim on the sleeves and hem of this easy-fitting jumper

next row: patt 18(19:20) sts.
Fasten off.

SLEEVES.—With 4 mm (8) hook make 74(78:82) ch, 1 tr in 5th ch from hook, 1 tr in next 3(5:1) ch, miss 1 tr, * 1 tr in each next 5 ch, 1 ch, miss 1 ch; rep from * ending with 5(7:3) tr, 3 turning ch.
Cont in patt and shape sides by inc 1 st at each end of every 4th row 6(5:4) times, then every foll alt row 0(2:4) times taking inc sts into pattern. Work a few rows on these 83(89:95) sts until sleeve measures 23 cm [9 inches] ending with a wrong side row.
SHAPE TOP.—next row: sl.st along 3 sts, patt to last 3 sts, 3 turning ch.
Dec 1 st at each end of next 6(7:8) rows.
Work 1 row on rem 83(89:95) sts.
Fasten off.

TO MAKE UP.—Join shoulder seams.
See ball band for pressing instructions.

NECK BORDER.—With right side facing, beg at left shoulder seam and work 1 row of dc round neck opening. Work a 2nd row of dc.
Fasten off.
Join ends of border.

FRINGE.—Cut a strip of thin cardboard 3 cm (1¼ inches].
With right side facing work 1 row of dc along foundation row of back, front and sleeves. Work a 2nd row of dc.
row 3: 1 dc in 1 st st, * hook into next st, place cardboard behind work holding it in left hand, take yarn round cardboard from front to back then over hook and draw a loop through st, yrh and draw through 2 loops to complete dc; rep from * along row, sliding cardboard along as required and slipping off loops, always leaving a few loops on card to anchor it.
Fasten off.
Insert sleeves joining shaped edges at top of sleeve to shaped edges of armhole at Back and Front and easing straight edge to fit. Join side and sleeve seams.
See ball band for pressing instructions.

row 2: sl.st over 7 sts, patt 18(19:20) sts.
Fasten off.
With right side facing, miss centre 21(23:25) sts, rejoin yarn to next st and patt to end. 25(26:27) sts.
next row: patt 18(19:20) sts.
Fasten off.

FRONT.—Work as given for Back until work measures 8 rows fewer than on Back have been worked to shoulder, ending with a wrong side row.
SHAPE NECK.—row 1: patt 32(33:34) sts, turn.
row 2: sl.st along 2 sts, pattern to end.
row 3: patt to last 2 sts, turn.
Rep rows 2 & 3 twice more.
row 8: sl.st along 2 sts, patt 18(19:20) sts.
Fasten off.
With right side facing, miss centre 7(9:11) sts, rejoin yarn to next st and patt to end. 32:33:34 sts.
Rep rows 3 & 2 three times.

V-NECK DRESS

1967

* An easy to wear, slightly waisted dress with three quarter length sleeves is knitted in stocking stitch and edged at its hem and V-neck with a crocheted shell lace pattern

MATERIALS.—Jaeger Matchmaker DK: 12(12:13) 50 g balls; 3.50 mm (9) crochet hook; pair 4 mm (8) knitting needles.
TENSION.—22 sts and 30 rows to 10 cm [4 inches] over st.st.
STITCHES.—1. stocking stitch; 2. crochet edging.
SIZES.—To fit dress sizes 8-10(12-14:16-18). Length 105.5 cm [41½ inches]; sleeve seam 28 cm [11 inches].

Figures in brackets () refer to larger sizes.
ABBREVIATIONS.—beg-begin(ing); ch-chain; dc-double crochet; dec-decrease; inc-increase; k-knit; p-purl; psso-pass slipped stitch over; rem-remaining; sl-slip; st(s)-stitch(es); st st-stocking stitch; tog-together; tr-treble; yrh-yarn round hook.

BACK.—With 4 mm (8) needles cast on 100(110:120) sts.
row 1: p.
row 2: k
Continue working in stocking stitch until work measures 51 cm [20 inches] from beg of work ending with a p row.
decrease row: k2, sl 1, k1, psso, work to last 4 sts, k2 tog, k2.
Repeat this row every 10th row four times more. 90(100:110) sts. Work straight until work measures 68.5 cm [27 inches] from beg of work ending with a p row.
Mark for waistline. Work 10 rows straight.
increase row: k2, inc 1 st in next st by k an extra st in back of st in row below, k to last 3 sts, inc 1 st as before, k to end. 92(102:112) sts. Repeat inc row every 10th row twice more. 96(106:114) sts. Work straight until work measures 18 cm [7 inches] from waistline marker ending with a p row.
SHAPE ARMHOLES.—Cast off 6 sts at beg of next 2 rows. Dec 1 st each end of next row then every other row until there are 74(78:82) sts. Work straight until armhole measures 19(20:20) cm [7½(7½:8) inches].
SHAPE SHOULDERS.—Cast off 8(8:9) sts at beg of next 2 rows. Cast off 7(8:8) sts at beg of next 4 rows. 30(30:32) sts.
Cast off rem sts.

FRONT.—Work as for Back until 2 rows above last inc row and ending with a k row. 96(106:114) sts.
Dividing row: p 45(50:54) sts, sl these sts on to a st holder for right front, cast off 6(6:6) sts for centre front, p across rem sts.

LEFT FRONT.—Work 4 rows straight.
row 5: k to within 3 sts of front edge, k2 tog, k1.
Repeat neck dec every 6th row 10 times shaping armhole as for back when 18 cm [7 inches] above waistline. 22(24:25) sts. Work straight until front measures same as back to shoulder shaping.
SHAPE SHOULDER.—Cast off 8(8:9) sts once and 7(8:8) sts every other row twice.

RIGHT FRONT.—With wrong side of work facing, sl the 45(50:54) sts from holder on to a needle. Beg at centre front, work four rows straight.
row 5: k1, sl 1, k1, psso and work to end.
Finish this side to match Left Front.

SLEEVES.—With 4 mm (8) needles cast on 47(51:53) sts. Beg with a p row work 5 rows in st st, k next row inc 7(7:7) sts evenly spaced across row. 54(58:60) sts.
K 1 row inserting needle in back loops of sts for turning ridge. K 1 row and continue in st st for 5 more rows.
Inc 1 st at each end of next row then every 5(5:5) cm [2(2:2) inches] four times more. 64(68:70) sts.
Work straight until work measures 28 cm [11 inches] from ridge ending with a p row.
SHAPE SLEEVE.—Cast off 6 sts at beg of next 2 rows. Dec 1 st at each end of next row then every other row 6 times, every 4th row 4 times then every other row twice, every row 4 times. 20(22:24) sts.
Cast off.

MAKING UP.—Sew seams. Sew in sleeves. Turn hems to wrong side and sew.
See ball band for pressing instructions.

NECK EDGING.—With 3.50 mm (9) hook and right side facing, work 13 dc from centre back neck to left shoulder seam, 38 dc along left side edge of neck to beg of V neck, draw up a loop at corner and in first st cast off, yrh, draw through all loops, work 4 dc on centre

cast off sts, draw up a loop in last st cast off and 1 loop at corner, yrh, draw through all loops, work dc on right side edge of neck and to centre back to correspond with left side. (108 dc).
row 1: * ch 3, miss 2 dc, 1 dc in next dc; repeat from * to end joining with a sl.st in first ch.
row 2: work 5 tr in first 3 ch space, * 1 dc in next 3 ch space, 5 tr in next 3 ch space; repeat from * to end ending with 1 dc in last 3 ch space.
row 3: * ch 3, 1 dc in third tr of shell, ch 3, 1 dc in dc; repeat from * to end.
row 4: work 5 dc in first 3 ch space, * 1 dc in next space, 5 dc in next space; repeat from * to end joining with a sl.st.
Fasten off.

HEM EDGING.—With right side facing, work 198 dc around lower edge of dress. Work 4 rows as for neck edge.
Fasten off.

EDGED WAISTCOAT

1979

* Quick to make sleeveless waistcoat with front points worked in reverse stocking stitch and chunky wool. Double crochet is used to edge the front and hem edges, and to make the mock pockets

MATERIALS.—Wendy Kintyre: 7(7:8:9) 50 g balls; 5 mm (6) crochet hook; pair 5½ mm (5) knitting needles; 4 buttons.

TENSION.—15 sts and 21 rows to 10 cm [4 inches] over stocking stitch.

STITCHES.—1. reverse stocking stitch; 2. double crochet worked through back loops only.

SIZES.—To fit bust 81(86:91:96) cm [32(34:36:38) inches]. Actual measurements: 91(96:101:106) cm [36(37¾:39¾:42) inches]; length at centre back (including crochet border) 45(45:46:46) cm [17½(17½:18:18) inches].

Figures in brackets () refer to larger sizes.

ABBREVIATIONS.—alt-alternate; beg-beginning; ch-chain; cont-continue; dec-decrease; dc-double crochet; foll-following; inc-increase; k-knit; p-purl; rem-remaining; rep-repeat; rev st.st-reversed stocking st (p side is right side); sl.st-slip stitch; sts-stitches; tog-together.

BACK.—With 5½ mm (5) needles cast on 60(64:68:72) sts and beg with a p row work in rev st.st. When work measures 4 cm [1½ inches] inc 1 st at both ends of work. Inc 1 st at both ends when work measures 8 cm [3 inches], 12 cm [4¾ inches] and 16 cm [6¼ inches] from beg then cont on 68(72:76:80) sts until work measures 21 cm [8¼ inches] from beg ending with a k row.

SHAPE ARMHOLES.—Cast off 4 sts at beg of next 2 rows, 2 sts at beg of next 2(2:4:4) rows and 1 st at beg of next 8(10:8:10) rows. Cont on rem 48(50:52:54) sts until work measures 43(43:44:44) cm [17(17:17¼:17¼) inches] from beg ending with a k row.

SHAPE SHOULDER AND NECK.—Row 1: cast off 4 sts, p until there are 11(12:12:13) sts on right needle, leave these for right back, now cast off next 18(18:20:20) sts, p to end. Cont on 15(16:16:17) sts now rem on needle for left Back.

row 2: cast off 4, k to last 2 sts at neck edge, k 2 tog.

row 3: cast off 1 st, p to end.

row 4: as row 2.

row 5: p.

row 6: cast off rem 4(5:5:6) sts.

With wrong side facing rejoin yarn to neck edge of right back sts, cast off 1 st, k to end. next row: cast off 4 sts, p to last 2 sts, p2 tog. Cast off 1 st at beg of foll row.
Cast off rem 4(5:5:6) sts.

RIGHT FRONT.—With 5½ mm (5) needles cast on 2 sts and beg with a p row work in rev st.st shaping both edges.

For front shaping inc 1 st at front edge at end of wrong side rows on 2nd row then every foll 4th row 6 times in all. **At the same time** for side shaping cast on at beg of wrong side rows 2 sts eight times, 2(3:3:4) sts once and 3(4:6:7) sts once. When all incs have been completed cont on these 29(31:33:35) sts until work measures 4 cm [1½ inches] from the last casting on at side; inc 1 st at side edge on next row then at same edge at 4 cm [1½ inch] intervals three times more. Cont on 33(35:37:39) sts until work measures 21 cm [8¼ inches] at side edge, ending at this edge.
SHAPE ARMHOLE AND FRONT.—next

Crochet edging and mock pockets give a stylish air to this useful waistcoat

row: cast off 4 sts, k to last 2 sts, k2 tog. Cast off at armhole edge 2 sts on next 1(1:2:2) alt rows and 1 st on next 4(5:4:5) alt rows. **At the same time** dec 1 st at front edge at 3 row intervals twice more then at same edge on every foll 4th row 8(8:9:9) times more. Cont on rem 12(13:13:14) sts until armhole matches Back to shoulder, ending at armhole edge.
SHAPE SHOULDER.—Cast off 4 sts at beg of next row and next alt row. Work 1 row then cast off rem 4(5:5:6) sts.

LEFT FRONT.—Work as for Right Front working all shapings at opposite edge.

COMPLETION AND MOCK POCKETS.—Sew shoulder and side seams and press lightly.
With right side facing, join yarn at lower edge of right side seam. With 5 mm (6) hook, work 1 ch then work in dc all round entire front, neck and lower edges, join with a sl st to 1st ch, turn.
next row: work in back loops only of the dc of first row, working 2 dc into each of 2 adjacent sts at lower points and making four loops for buttonholes on right front; the upper one just below 1st dec and the lower one just above last inc with rem 2 evenly spaced. For each buttonhole work 2 ch and miss 2 dc. Work two more rows of dc always into back loops and working incs as before; join at end of last row and fasten off.
Similarly work 4 rows of dc round each armhole edge.

MOCK POCKETS.—With 5 mm (6) hook, make 15 ch, hook into second ch from hook and work 1 dc in this and all subsequent ch. Work four more rows of dc working in back loops only and turning with 1 ch.
Fasten off.
Press rev st.st and crochet borders. Sew mock pockets to fronts as illustrated. Sew on buttons.
See ball band for pressing instructions.

TWEED SHIRT

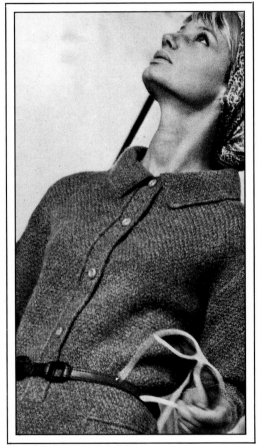

1964

* A fine wool tweed yarn and straightforward double crochet is used for this smart long sleeved, shirt-style jacket with collar and buttoned front panel and two neat banded pockets

MATERIALS.—Rowan Fine Tweed: 22(24:26:28) 25 g hanks; 2.50 mm (2) and 3.50 (9) crochet hooks; 5 buttons.
TENSION.—6 dc and 7 rows to 2.5 cm [1 inch] over double crochet.

STITCH.—double crochet
SIZES.—To fit bust 86(91:97:102) cm [34 (36:38:40) inches]. Actual measurement: bust 99(104:109:114) cm [39(41:43:45) inches]; length from shoulder 63.5(63.5:65:65) cm [25(25:26:26) inches]; sleeve seam: 41 cm [16 inches].
Figures in brackets () refer to larger sizes.
ABBREVIATIONS.—alt-alternate; ch-chain; dc-double crochet; dec-decrease; inc-increase; sl.st-slip stitch; st(s)-stitch(es); yrh-yarn round hook.

BACK.—With 2.50 mm (2) hook, make 121(127:133:139) ch, yrh, hook into 2nd ch from hook and work 1 dc in this and all subsequent ch to end of row, 1 turning ch. 120(126:132:138) sts.
Cont in dc and work straight for 41 cm [16 inches].
SHAPE ARMHOLE.—Work to last 3 sts, turn.
next row: work to last 3 sts, turn
next row: work to last 2 sts, turn
Repeat this last row until there are 96(102:108:114) sts.
Work straight until armhole measures 23(23:25.5:25.5) cm [9(9:10:10) inches].
SHAPE SHOULDERS.—Sl.st across 11(12:13:14) sts, work to last 11(12:13:14) sts, turn.
Repeat this row twice more. 30 sts remain.
Fasten off.

POCKET LININGS.—(work two) With 2.50 mm (2) hook, make 31 ch, hook into 2nd ch from hook and work 1 dc in this and all subsequent ch to end of row. (30 sts).
Work in dc until work measures 9.5 cm [3¾ inches].
Fasten off.

FRONT.—With 2.50 mm (2) hook, make 121(127:133:139) ch, hook into 2nd ch from hook and work 1 dc in this and all subsequent ch to end of row, 1 turning ch.

Working in dc work straight for 13 cm [5 inches].

next row: work 15(16:17:18) sts, sl.st across 30 sts, work next 30(34:38:42) sts, sl.st across 30 sts, work 15(16:17:18) sts.

next row: work 15(16:17:18) sts, work across sts of pocket lining, work next 30(34:38:42) sts, work across sts of pocket lining, work 15(16:17:18) sts. Work another 5 rows.

LEFT FRONT.—Work 66(69:72:75) sts, turn. Finish this side first.

Cont in dc until work measures 41 cm [16 inches] from beg ending at armhole edge.

SHAPE ARMHOLE.—Sl.st across 3 sts, work to end.

next row: work to last 2 sts, turn.

Cont dec 2 sts at armhole edge until there are 55(58:61:64) sts.

Work straight until armhole measures 19(19:20:20) cm [7½(7½:8:8) inches] keeping armhole edge straight and ending at neck edge at last row.

SHAPE NECK.—sl.st across 12 sts, dec 2tog, work to end.

Dec 2tog at neck edge on this and every alt row until there are 33(36:39:42) sts.

Work straight until armhole measures same as for Back.

SHAPE SHOULDER.—next row: work to last 11 sts, turn.

next row: work to last 11 sts.

Fasten off.

RIGHT FRONT.—Join yarn to front edge and work across rem 54(57:60:63) sts. Work straight until work measures 41 cm [16 inches] and ending at armhole edge.

SHAPE ARMHOLE.—Sl.st across 3 sts, work to end.

next row: work to last 2 sts, turn.

Repeat last row until there are 41(44:47:50) sts.

Work until armhole measures 19(19:20:20) cm [7½(7½:8:8) inches].

SHAPE NECK.—Dec 2tog at neck edge on this and every alt row until 33(36:39:42) sts remain, ending at armhole edge.

Work straight until armhole measures same as for Back.

SHAPE SHOULDER.—Work as for left front.

FRONT BAND.—With 2.50 mm (2) hook, make 106(106:112:112) ch, hook in second ch from hook and work 1 dc in this and all subsequent ch to end of row, 1 turning ch.

Continue in dc and work 6 rows.

BUTTONHOLE ROW.—Work 6(6:7:7) sts, * sl.st over 4 sts, work 18(18:19:19) sts; repeat this three more times, sl.st over 4 sts, 7(7:8:8) sts.

next row: work 7(7:8:8) sts, * 4 ch over sl. sts, 18(18:19:19) sts; repeat from * to end.

next row: work in dc working 4 dc in 4 ch space.

Work 5 more rows.

Fasten off.

SLEEVES.—With 2.50 mm (2) hook, make 57(57:63:63) ch, hook in 2nd ch from hook and work 1 dc in this and all subsequent ch to end of work, 1 turning ch.

Continue in dc and work 4 rows.

Inc 1 st either side on every 8th row until there are 78(78:84:84) sts.

Work until sleeve measures 41 cm [16 inches].

SHAPE TOP.—Sl.st across 3 sts, work to last 3 sts, turn.

next row: sl.st across 2 sts, work to last 2 sts, turn.

Dec 1 st at each end of next and every alt row until there are 26(26:32:32) sts.

Dec 2tog at each end of every row until 14(14:20:20) sts remain.

Fasten off.

COLLAR.—With 2.50 mm (2) hook, make approximately 130(130:150:150) ch and work 3 rows of dc. * Change to 3.50 (9) hook and work 4 rows. Cont in dc inc 1 st at each end of next and every alt row until work measures 7.5 cm [3 inches] from *.

Fasten off.

POCKET FLAPS.—With 2.50 mm (2) hook, work 1 dc in each of 30 sts then work in dc for 5 cm [2 inches].

Fasten off.

TO MAKE UP.—Sew shoulder seams, set in sleeves. Sew side and sleeve seams. Sew down pocket linings. With 2.50 mm (2) hook, sl.st. along main 3 sides of collar and all sides of front band and pocket flaps. Pin front band to right front edge, overlapping the band by one st of right side. Sew in place. Sew lower end over underlap. Sew edge of collar to neck to within 2.5 cm [1 inch] of front edges. Sew down pocket flaps. Sew the five buttons in position.

See ball band for pressing instructions.

SPORTS PULLOVER

1 9 5 7

* *This man's loose-fitting sports sweater with long sleeves and wide collar is worked in a 4 ply wool and double double crochet. The sleeve cuffs are worked in crocheted treble rib*

MATERIALS.—Jaeger Matchmaker 4 ply: 13(14:15:16) 50 g balls; 4 mm (8) crochet hook.

TENSION.—7 sts and 6 spaces over 5 cm [2 inches] of stitch 2.

STITCHES.—1. treble rib; 2. double double crochet.

SIZES.—To fit chest 97(102:107:112) cm [38(40:42:44) inches]. Actual measurements 112(117:122:127) cm [44(46:48:50) inches]; length from shoulder 68(69:69:70) cm [$26\frac{3}{4}$(27:$27\frac{1}{4}$:$27\frac{1}{2}$) inches]; sleeve seam 52 cm [$20\frac{1}{2}$ inches].

Figures in brackets () refer to larger sizes.

ABBREVIATIONS.—alt-alternate; ch-chain; cont-continue; dc-double crochet; double dc-double double crochet; dec-decrease; inc-increase; patt-pattern; rb/tr-yarn round hook, hook from behind and from right to left round stem of stitch and complete in usual way; rf/tr, yarn round hook, hook from front and from right to left round stem of stitch and complete in usual way; rep-repeat; sl.st-slip stitch; st(s)-stitch(es); yrh-yarn round hook.

BACK.—With 4 mm (8) hook, make 145(153:159:167) ch, yrh, hook in 3rd ch from hook and work 1 tr in this and all subsequent ch to end, 2 turning ch. 143(151:157:165) sts.

row 1: miss first st, * 1 rf/tr in first st, 1 rb/tr in next st; rep from * to end, 2 turning ch.

Row 1 forms rib pattern. Work 5 cm [2 inches] in pattern. Change to second pattern stitch.

row 1: hook in first st, yrh, draw through a loop, yrh and draw through a loop, yrh and draw a loop through both loops on hook (one double dc worked), * 1 ch, miss 1 st, 1 double dc in next st; rep from * to end of row.

row 2: * 1 double dc in ch space, 1 ch; rep from * to end.

Rows 1 & 2 form pattern. Cont in pattern until work measures 46 cm [18 inches].

SHAPE ARMHOLES.—Sl.st across 7 sts, work to last 7 sts, turn.

Dec 1 st at each end of row 9 times. ** work straight until armholes measure 22(23:23.5:24) cm [$8\frac{3}{4}$(9:$9\frac{1}{4}$:$9\frac{1}{2}$) inches].

SHAPE SHOULDERS.—Sl.st across 9(10:10:11) sts, work to last 9(10:10:11) sts, turn. Do this three more times. 39(39:45:45) sts.

FRONT.—Work as for Back to **.

DIVIDE FOR NECK.—Patt across 62(66:69:73) sts, turn. Finish this side first. Work in patt until armhole measures 16.5 cm [$6\frac{1}{2}$ inches] ending at armhole edge.

next row: patt 48(52:55:59) sts, turn.

Dec 2 sts at neck edge on every alternate row until there are 36(40:40:44) sts. Cont straight until armhole measures same as for Back, ending at armhole edge.

SHAPE SHOULDER.—Sl.st across 9(10: 10:11) sts, work to end. Work to last 9(10: 10:11) sts, turn. Repeat these two rows once more.

SECOND SIDE.—Make 16 ch, 1 double dc in 3rd ch from hook, work in patt to last but one ch, 1 ch, 1 double dc in next unworked space on Front, patt across remaining sts, turn. 62(66:69:73) sts.

Complete as for first Front.

Join shoulder seams.

Starting at Front neck opening and with wrong side facing, work 3 dc to every 2 rows round neck opening.

Fasten off.

SLEEVES.—With 4 mm (8) hook, make 69(71:73:75) ch, yrh, hook in 3rd ch from hook and work 1 tr in this and all subsequent ch to end. Work 5 cm [2 inches] in rib pattern. Cont in main pattern inc 1 st either side on next and every 4th row until there are 109(111:111:113) sts. Work straight until sleeve measures 52 cm [20½ inches].

SHAPE TOP.—Sl.st over 7 sts, work to last 7 sts, turn.

Dec 1 st either side of next alt 7 rows then dec 1 st either side of next 16 rows.

next row: sl.st across 4 sts, work to last 4 sts, turn.

next row: sl.st across 5 sts, work to last 5 sts, turn.

next row: sl.st across 6 sts, work to last 6 sts. Fasten off.

COLLAR.—With 4 mm (8) hook, make 63 ch, yrh, hook in 3rd ch from hook and work in double dc patt to end.

next row: work in patt to end, 10 ch.

next row: incorporating 10 ch in pattern, work in patt to end, 10 ch. Rep this row once more.

Work straight for 9 cm [3½ inches] ending with a wrong side row. Work 1 row of dc round collar.

Fasten off.

TO MAKE UP.—Sew sleeves to armholes. Sew side and sleeve seams. Sew collar to neck and sew underlap in place.

See ball band for pressing instructions.

Shell pattern panels, collar and sleeves feature on this simple, loose-fitting cardigan

RIGHT FRONT PANEL.—Work as for Left Front reversing edging and neck shaping and working buttonholes as given to correspond with marked button positions.
WORK BUTTONHOLES.—row 1: k3, cast off 2 sts , k to end.
row 2: cast on 2 sts over those cast off in row 1.

RIGHT BACK SIDE PANEL.—With 3 mm (10) hook, make 37(40:43:46:49) ch, yrh, hook in 4th chain from hook and work 1 tr, * miss 2 ch, 2 tr in next ch; rep from * to end, 3 turning ch.
row 1: 2 tr in first tr, * miss next tr, 3 tr in first tr of next group; rep from * to end, 3 turning ch. [12(13:14:15:16) 3 tr groups].
row 2: 1 tr in centre of first group, * 2 tr in centre tr of next group; rep from * to end, 3 turning ch. 12(13:14:15:16) 3 tr groups.
These 2 rows form pattern.
Cont in patt until panel measures 42 cm [16½ inches] ending after row 1 of patt.
SHAPE ARMHOLE.—Patt over 8(8:9:9:9) groups, turn and cont on these sts only. Cont in patt until armhole measures 18(19:20: 21:22) cm [7(7½:7¾:8¼:8¾) inches] ending after row 1 of patt.
SHAPE SHOULDER.—Work 4 pattern groups and fasten off.

LEFT BACK SIDE PANEL.—As for Right Back panel to armhole.
SHAPE ARMHOLE.—next row: sl.st over 4(5:5:6:7) groups, patt to end.

Complete to match right side Back panel reversing shapings.

LEFT FRONT SIDE PANEL.—Work as for Right Back.

RIGHT FRONT SIDE PANEL.—Work as for Left Back.

SLEEVES.—With 3 mm (10) hook make 61(61:64:64:67) ch. Work as side panel having 20(20:21:21:22) groups. Work 4 rows ending with row 1 of patt.
first inc row: 1 tr in last tr of preceding row, 2 tr in next st, * 2 tr in centre of next group; rep from * to last group, 2 tr in centre st, 2 tr in top of turning ch, 3 turning ch. (2 groups increased.)
Cont to inc 1 group at both ends of every 4th row until there are 28(28:29:29:30) groups then on every alt row until there are 32(34:35:37:38) groups. Cont straight until sleeve measures 37 cm [14½ inches].
Mark both ends of last row.
SHAPE TOP.—next row: sl.st over 5 groups, 3 ch, patt to last 6 groups, sl.st in next group, 3 turning ch.
Rep last row once more and fasten off.

COLLAR.—With 3 mm (10) hook make 128(134:137:140:143) ch, yrh, hook into 2nd ch from hook and work 1 dc in this and all subsequent ch to end, 1 turning ch.
next row: 1 dc in each st to end, 2 turning ch.
next row: 2 tr in last dc of preceding row, * miss 2 dc, 3 tr in next dc; rep from * to end, 3 turning ch.
Cont in pattern and work 4 rows.
Fasten off.

TO MAKE UP.—Sew back panels together wth garter st edges overlapping one crochet st. Sew front panels in same way. Sew shoulder seams. Sew top of sleeves to straight edge of armholes sewing rows above markers to groups at underarm. Sew side and sleeve seams. Work 1 row dc round crochet parts of lower edge and sleeves. Face front panels and lower edges with ribbon. Cut matching buttonholes and buttonhole stitch ribbon and knitting together. Sew collar to neck edge. Sew on buttons.
See ball band for pressing instructions.

summertime

CARDIGAN BLOUSE

1954

*** Easy-fitting cardigan blouse with contrast edges,
sailor style collar and elbow-length sleeves worked in a
simple textured pattern. The ribbed welts are also
worked in crochet*

MATERIALS.—Sirdar Wash'n'Wear 4 ply
Crepe: 7(8:8:9) 50 g balls Main colour; 1 50 g
ball Contrast colour; 2.50 mm (2) crochet
hook; 8 buttons; 1 metre [39 inches] 2.5 cm [1
inch] wide ribbon (optional).
TENSION.—12½ patterns in stitch 2 to 10.5
cm [4¼ inches] in width.
STITCHES.—1. Ridge pattern; 2. Cluster
pattern.
SIZES.—To fit bust 81(86:91:96) cm
[32(34:36:38) inches]. Actual measurements:
100(107:114:121) cm [39½(42¼:45:47½) inches];
length 53.5(56:57:60) cm [21(22:22½:23½)
inches]; sleeve seam 11.5 cm [4½ inches]
excluding turn-back cuff.
Figures in brackets () refer to larger sizes.
ABBREVIATIONS.—C-contrast; ch-chain;
cont-continue; dc-double crochet; dec-
decrease; inc-increase; M-main; rem-remaining; rep-repeat; sl-slip; st(s)-stitch(es); tr-
treble; yrh-yarn round hook.

BACK.—Begin with welt. With M and 2.50
mm (2) hook make 26 ch, yrh, put hook into
2nd ch from hook and work 1 dc in this and all
subsequent ch to end of row, 1 turning ch.
row 1: 1 dc through both loops of first st, 1 dc
in back loop of next 23 sts, 1 dc in both loops
of last st, 1 turning ch.
Repeat row 1 until there are 52(56:60:64)
ridges. Do not break yarn.
Work alongside long side of welt with * (1 dc,
1 tr) in top st of next rib; rep from * to end, 1
turning ch. (52:56:60:64 patterns). This forms
right side of work.
Change to cluster pattern.
row 1: * miss 1 tr, (1 dc, 1 tr) in next dc; rep
from * to end, 1 turning ch.
This row forms pattern.
Continue in pattern and work 10 rows more.
First inc row: 1 dc in first tr, * (1 dc, 1 tr) in
next dc; rep from * to last pattern, (1 dc, 1 tr)
in next tr, 1 dc in last dc, 1 turning ch.
Second inc row: (1 dc, 1 tr) in first dc, work in
patt to last single dc, (1 dc, 1 tr) in last st.
(54:58:62:66 patterns).
Work 10 rows straight in pattern then rep the
2 inc rows. (56:60:64:68 patterns).
Work should measure 44.5(48:51:55) cm
[17½(19:20:21½) inches] in width.
Cont straight in patt until work measures
35.5(37:37:38) cm [14(14½:14½:15) inches].
SHAPE ARMHOLES.—First dec row: miss
first tr, 1 dc in next dc, miss next tr, (1 dc, 1 tr)
in next dc, work to last pattern, 1 dc in last dc,
1 turning ch.
Second dec row: miss first dc and tr, (1 dc, 1 tr)
in next dc, work to last pattern, miss 1 tr, 1 dc
in next dc, 1 tr in last dc.
One pattern now dec at each end.
Rep last 2 rows until 44(46:48:50) patterns
rem.
Cont straight until work measures 18(19:
20.5:21.5) cm [7(7½:8:8½) inches] from beg of

armhole shaping.

SHAPE SHOULDERS.—row 1: sl.st over first 2(3:3:4) patterns, 1 ch, pattern until 2(3:3:4) patterns rem, 1 sl.st into next tr, 1 turning ch.

row 2: miss sl.st, then sl.st over 4 patterns, 1 ch, pattern until 4 patterns rem, 1 sl.st in next tr, 1 turning ch.

Repeat last row twice. 16(16:18:18) patterns for back neck edge.

Fasten off.

LEFT FRONT.—With M and 2.50 mm (2) hook make 26 ch. Work welt as for Back until there are 33(35:37:39) ridges. Work next row as for Back. 33(35:37:39) patterns.

Change to pattern stitch 2 and work 11 rows in pattern.

Inc 1 pattern at side edge on next 2 rows, then inc 1 pattern at side edge on following 11th and 12th rows. 35(37:39:41) patterns.

Work should measure approx 27(28.5:30.5: 32.5)cm [10½(11¼:12:12¾) inches].

Cont straight in patt until work measures same as Back to armholes, ending at side edge.

SHAPE ARMHOLE.—Dec 1 pattern at side edge on every 2 rows as for Back, ie, begin first row as per first row on Back and end second row as per second row on Back until 26(27:28:29) patterns remain.

Cont straight in pattern until work measures same as Back to shoulders, ending at centre front edge.

SHAPE SHOULDER.—row 1: work to last 2(3:3:4) patterns, 1 sl.st in next tr, 1 turning ch.

row 2: miss sl.st, work in pattern to end, 1 turning ch.

row 3: work to last 4 patterns, 1 sl.st in next tr, 1 turning ch.

row 4: as row 2.

Rep last 2 rows twice. 12(12:13:13) patterns.

Fasten off but do not break yarn.

RIGHT FRONT.—With M and 2.50 mm (2) hook make 26 ch, work welt as for Back, making 2 buttonholes as follows:

Work 4 rows.

row 5: 2 dc, 4 ch, miss 4 dc, work 13 dc, 4 ch, miss 4 dc, dc in last 2 sts.

row 6: work 4 dc into each 4 ch space.

Place a marker up left front to mark further 6 buttonholes, the 6th 2.5 cm [1 inch] below beg of armhole shaping, the remaining 5 spaced equally between.

Now complete as for left front, reversing all shaping and working buttonholes when markers are reached as follows:

Front edge, work 2 patterns, 4 ch, miss 2 patterns, work to end.

On next row, work 2 patterns in each 4 ch space.

NOTE: When working armhole shaping, end at front edge and then dec as given for end of rows on back armhole shaping, and begin rows as on back armhole shaping.

SLEEVES.—With M and 2.50 mm (2) hook make 66(70:74:76) ch.

row 1: 1 dc in third ch from hook (forming 1 pattern), * miss 1 ch, (1 dc, 1 tr) in next ch; rep from * to end. 32(34:36:38) patterns.

Cont in pattern until work measures 5 cm [2 inches].

Inc 1 pattern at both ends of next 2 rows, then work 2 rows straight.

Rep these 4 rows until there are 40(42:44:46) patterns.

Cont straight until sleeve measures 16.5 cm [6½ inches] or 5 cm [2 inches] more than desired length.

SHAPE TOP.—Dec 1 pattern at both ends of next 2 rows, then work 2 rows straight.

Rep last 4 rows 1(1:2:2) times, then dec 1 pattern at both ends of every 2 rows until 28(30:30:32) patterns remain.

Next row: sl.st over first 2 patterns, work to last 2 patterns, turn.

Rep last row 3 times more.

Fasten off.

COLLAR.—Join shoulder seams. With M and 2.50 mm (2) hook, pick up yarn on left side of neck. Work 1 pattern into each pattern across top of rever to shoulder, across back neck edge and across other rever. Work in pattern for 7.5 cm [3 inches].

Fasten off.

EDGING.—With 2.50 mm (2) hook, join C to lower edge of right front and work in pattern up right front, round collar and down left front, working 1 pattern into every 2 row ends up fronts and 1 pattern into each pattern across collar and 2 patterns into each 'point' of collar.

Work a further row then fasten off.

SLEEVE EDGING.—With 2.50 mm (2) hook, join C to ch edge on one sleeve and work 2 rows in pattern.

Fasten off.

TO MAKE UP.—Set in sleeves. Join side and sleeve seams. Sew on buttons. If desired, face fronts with ribbon. Turn cuffs to right side. See ball band for pressing instructions.

Bikini

1972

* *Based on triangular motifs, this bikini is made in a high twist acrylic yarn. The top is joined with narrow ties and the briefs are worked in trebles from each side of the main motif*

MATERIALS.—Twilley's Galaxia 3: 2(2) 100 g balls; 2.50 mm (13) crochet hook; 1 metre (1 yard) elastic.
TENSION.—6 sts to 2.5 cm [1 inch].
STITCHES.—1. trebles; 2. openwork motif.
SIZES.—To fit bust 86(91) cm [34(36) inches]; to fit hip 91(97) cm [36(38) inches].

Figures in brackets () refer to larger sizes.
ABBREVIATIONS.—ch-chain; dc-double crochet; inc-increase; rep-repeat; sl.st-slip stitch; st(s)-stitch(es); tr-treble.

BRIEFS.—** With 2.50 mm (13) hook make 6 ch and join into a circle with sl.st.
round 1: 2 ch, * in circle work 3 tr but keep last loop of each tr on hook, then draw a loop through all loops on hook [1 cluster made], 5 ch; rep from * twice more.
round 2: * 1 dc in cluster, 3 ch, (3 tr, 3 ch, 3 tr, 3ch) in ch loop of round 1; rep from * twice more.
round 3: 1 dc in ch loop, 3 ch, * in ch loop between 3 tr groups work (3 tr, 3 ch, 3 tr, 3 ch), in next ch loop work (1 dc, 3 ch, 1 dc, 3 ch); rep from * twice more.
round 4: * 1 tr in each tr, (2 tr, 3 ch, 2 tr) in ch loop, 1 tr in each tr, 3 ch, 1 tr in next ch loop, 1 cluster in next ch loop, 1 tr in next ch loop, 3 ch; rep from * twice more.
round 5: * 1 tr in each tr, (2tr, 3 ch, 2 tr) in ch loop, 1 tr in each tr, 3 ch, 1 dc in next ch loop, 3 ch, 1 dc in next ch loop, 3 ch; rep from * twice more. **
Rep rounds 4 and 5 twice more then round 4, once. Work 1 dc in next tr, 2 turning ch.
next row: 2 tr in ch loop, 1 tr in tr, 1 tr in cluster, 1 tr in tr, 1 tr in ch loop, 1 tr in each tr, 2 tr in ch loop, 2 turning ch. 25 sts.
row 1: 1 tr in each st to end, 2 turning ch.
row 2: miss first st, 1 tr in each st to end, 2 turning ch.
Rep rows 1 and 2 five times more, 2 turning ch.
For 91 cm [36 inches] size only: Work 2 rows straight, 2 turning ch.
All sizes: next row: 1 tr in each st to last st, 2 tr in last st, 2 turning ch.
next row: 2 tr in first st, 1 tr in each st to last st, 2 tr in last st, 2 turning ch.
Rep last 2 rows six times more. 40 sts.
Keeping waist edge straight, continue to inc 1 tr on every row at leg edge until there are

51(53) sts ending at leg edge, turn with 26 ch.

row 1: 1 tr in 3rd ch from hook, 1 tr in each st to end, 2 turning ch.

row 2: 1 tr in each st to last 6 sts, 1 dc in next st, 1 sl.st in next st, 1 turning ch.

row 3: sl.st in each next 4 sts, 1 dc in next st, 1 tr in each st to end, 2 turning ch.

row 4: 1 tr in each st to last 3 tr sts, 2 turning ch.

row 5: 1 tr in each st to end, 2 turning ch.

row 6: 1 tr in each st to end, 9 turning ch.

row 7: 1 dc in 2nd ch from hook, 1 dc in each next 4 sts, 1 tr in each st to end, 2 turning ch.

row 8: 1 tr in each st to last st, 1 dc in last st, 5 turning ch.

row 9: 1 dc in 2nd ch from hook, 1 tr in each st to end, 2 turning ch.

row 10: 1 tr in each st to last 24 sts, 2 turning ch.

row 11: miss first st, 1 tr in each st to end, 2 turning ch.

row 12: 1 tr in each st to last 2 sts, miss 1 st, 1 tr in last st, 2 turning ch.

Rep rows 11 and 12 4(5) times more then row 11 once. Turn with 2 ch. 40 sts.

next row: miss first st, 1 tr in each st to last 2 sts, miss 1 st, 1 tr in last st, 2 turning ch.

next row: miss first st, 1 tr in each st to end, 2 turning ch.

Rep last 2 rows six times more, 2 turning ch.

For size 91 cm [36 inches] only: Work 2 rows straight, 2 turning ch.

All sizes: next row: 1 tr in each st to last st, 2 tr in last st, 2 turning ch.

next row: 1 tr in each st to end, 2 turning ch.

Rep last 2 rows five times more. 25 sts.

Cut yarn and fasten off.

TO MAKE UP.—Oversew the last 25 sts to the opposite edge of the centre motif. Oversew the shaped edges of the crotch piece to the two remaining edges of the centre motif. Work a row of firm dc round leg, ending with 1 ch.

Do not turn but work another row of dc right round, working from left to right instead of from right to left.

Cut yarn and fasten off.

Work round other leg in same way. Work a row of dc round waist, working over the elastic at the same time. Secure elastic firmly. Press lightly.

TOP.— Work motif as given for Briefs from ** to **.

For size 86 cm [34 inches] only: Rep rounds 4 and 5 twice more.

For size 91 cm [36 inches] only: Rep rounds 4 and 5 twice more, round 4 once.

next round: * 1 dc in each tr, 3 dc in corner ch loop, 1 dc in each tr, 1 dc in ch loop, 1 dc in cluster, 1 dc in ch loop; rep from * twice more. Join with a sl.st, work 1 ch then work another row of dc right round but working from left to right instead of from right to left.

Cut yarn and fasten off.

Work another motif in same way.

TIES.—Work 2 ch, hook in 2nd ch from hook and draw up a loop, then draw another loop through both sts on hook.

next row: Hook into 2nd st from hook and draw up a loop then draw a loop through both sts on hook. Rep last row for 127 cm [50 inches].

Cut yarn and fasten off.

Work another tie in same way.

TO MAKE UP.—Sew one corner of each motif together. Press lightly. Attach a tie to each motif at top corner. Thread tie through remaining corners in opposite motifs.

T-SHIRT

1953

* A long line, loose-fitting T-shirt with narrow contrast stripes carefully matched at side and sleeve and a simple, squared neck. It is worked in a medium-weight cotton in half trebles

MATERIALS.—Twilley's Lyscordet: 16(17: 17) 25 g balls Main colour; 7(8:8) 25 g balls Contrast colour; 2 mm (1) crochet hook.
TENSION.—5 htr and 4 spaces to 2.5 cm [1 inch] over stitch 1.
STITCH.—1. half trebles.
SIZES.—To fit bust 81(86:91) cm [32(34:36) inches]. Actual measurements: 99(105.5: 110.5) cm [39(41½:43½) inches]; length 66(66: 69) cm [26(26:27) inches]; sleeve seam 33(33:

33) cm [13(13:13) inches].
Figures in brackets () refer to larger sizes.
ABBREVIATIONS.—ch-chain; C-Contrast colour; dec-decrease; htr-half treble; M-Main colour; rep-repeat; yrh-yarn round hook.

BACK.—With M and 2 mm (1) hook make 178(188:198) ch, yrh, put hook into the third ch from the hook and work 1 htr, * 1 ch, miss 1 ch, 1 htr in next ch; rep from * to end, 2 turning ch. This is the foundation row.
next row: 1 htr in first 1 ch space, * 1 ch, 1 htr in next space; rep from * to end, 2 turning ch. This row forms pattern.
Continue in pattern working 5 rows in M, 2 rows in C alternately.
Work to end of 15th C colour stripe.
SHAPE ARMHOLES.—Dec 1 space and 1 htr at end of every row until 23(23:24) C stripes have been worked.
Fasten off.

FRONT.—Work as for Back.

SLEEVES.—With C, make 118(126:134) ch. Work as for Back for 6 rows, then increase 1 space and 1 htr at end of next 2 rows, keeping the colour sequence. Rep last 8 rows four times. Work to end of 12th C stripe.
SHAPE TOP.—Dec 1 space and 1 htr at end of every row until 20(20:21) C stripes have been worked.
Fasten off.

TO MAKE UP.—Sew raglan seams matching stripes. Sew side and sleeve seams. Press lightly.

BOAT-NECKED SHIRT

1956

* Loose-fitting boat-necked short sleeved T-shirt with contrast rib at neck, cuffs and welts. The main parts are worked in double crochet with contrast stripes and the edgings are in stocking stitch

MATERIALS.—Twilley's Stalite 9(10:11) 50 g balls Main colour; 5(5:5) 50 g balls Contrast colour; 3.50 mm (9) crochet hook; pair of 3 mm (11) knitting needles.
TENSION.—7 sts to 4 cm [1½ inches] over stitch 2.
STITCHES.—1. stocking stitch; 2. double crochet.
SIZES.—To fit chest 96(102:107) cm [38(40:42) inches]. Actual measurements: 108(115.5:121) cm [42½(45½:47½) inches]; length 67(69:70) cm [26½(27:27½) inches];

sleeve seam 25(25.5:26) cm [10(10:10¼) inches]
Figures in brackets () refer to larger sizes.
ABBREVIATIONS.—beg-beginning; ch-chain; C-contrast colour; cont-continue; dc-double crochet; dec-decrease; inc-increase; k-knit; M-main colour; p-purl; rep-repeat; sl.st-slip stitch; st(s)-stitch(es); st.st-stocking stitch; tog-together.

BACK.—With 3 mm (11) needles and C, cast on 123(132:138) sts loosely. Work 12 rows in st.st ending with a p row.
With right side of work facing and using a second ball of yarn, make hem. Pick up and k 1 st from each st cast on, place the 2 needles side by side and using another 3 mm (11) needle, * k tog 1 st from each needle; repeat from * to end. Turn, p3, *p2 tog, p3; repeat from * to end. 100(106:111) sts.
next row: using M and 3.50 mm (9) hook, put hook through first st on needle and make 2 ch, drop st from needle, * hook into next st on needle and pull loop through, yarn round hook and pull through 2 loops on hook, drop st from needle; repeat from * to end of row.
Work 4 rows in dc using M and 2 rows in C. Repeat these 6 rows throughout. When work measures 42(43:44) cm [16½(17:17½) inches] or length required, shape armhole.
SHAPE ARMHOLE.—sl.st across 5 sts and work to last 5 sts, turn.
Now dec 1 dc at the beg and end of next 3 rows.
Cont in pattern until armhole measures 25.5(26:26.5) cm [10(10¼:10½) inches].
Using C and 3 mm (11) needles, * pick up and k 1 st in the next 3 dc, pick up 2 sts in next dc, 1 st in next 2 dc and 2 sts in next dc; repeat from * along the row.
SHAPE SHOULDER.—Cast off 8(9:9) sts at the beg of the next 4 rows. Cast off 9(9:10) sts at beg of next 2 rows. Still using C, cont over the remaining sts for another 6 rows.
Cast off loosely.

FRONT.—Work as for Back.

SLEEVES.—With 3 mm (11) needles and C, cast on 102(106:106) sts and work the hem as given for Back. Change to M and using a 3.50 mm (9) hook, work in dc as given for Back. When 6 rows have been worked, inc 1 st at beg and end of each 6th row until side edge measures 25(25.5:26) cm [10(10:10¼) inches] ending on the same colour and row as for Front and Back. Sl.st over 5 dc and work to last 5 dc, 1 turning ch.

row 1: 1 dc in each dc to end, 1 turning ch.
row 2: miss first dc, work 1 dc in each dc to last dc, 1 turning ch. Rep row 2 until 28(30:32) rows have been worked.
Fasten off.

TO MAKE UP.—Fold last 6 rows of Front and Back to wrong side and stitch. Join shoulder seams. Set sleeves into armholes, matching stripes, and sew with back stitch. Join sleeve and side seams with back stitch. See ball band for pressing instructions.

SPOTTED BLOUSE

1935

** *Easy-fitting cardigan blouse with elbow-length sleeves and neat collar is patterned with a small spot design over trebles, using a cotton yarn. The ribbed welts are knitted*

MATERIALS.—DMC Hermina: 9 50 g balls Main colour; 2 50 g balls Contrast colour; pair 2¼ mm (13) knitting needles; 1.75 mm (2) crochet hook; 5 buttons.

TENSION.—8 sts (chain or tr) and 4 tr rows over 2.50 cm [1 inch] over stitch pattern 2.

STITCHES.—1. k2, p2 rib; 2. trebles; 3. double crochet worked in the back threads.

WORKING IN TWO COLOURS.—The Contrast cotton is carried behind the work all the time until it is needed and the Contrast spots are worked as they are reached. Before each change of colour, the Main thread is twisted around the Contrast.

The spots are worked as a 2 tr cluster as follows:

* 1 cluster (Contrast yrh, insert hook, draw up Contrast loop, yrh, draw through two Contrast loops), Contrast yrh, insert hook in same stitch, draw up Contrast loop, yrh, draw through 2 Contrast loops, Main yrh, draw through all 3 loops.

SIZES.—To fit bust 86–91 cm [34–36 inches]. Actual measurement 102 cm [40 inches]; length from shoulder 44 cm [17¼ inches]; sleeve seam 20 cm [8 inches].

ABBREVIATIONS.—alt-alternate; beg-beginning; C-Contrast colour; cont-continue; dc-double crochet; dec-decrease; foll-following; inc-increase; k-knit; M-Main colour; p-purl; sl.st-slip stitch; st(s)-stitch(es); tr-treble; yrh-yarn round hook.

LEFT FRONT.—With 2¼ mm (13) knitting needles and M cast on 86 sts and k into the back of the sts. Work 7.5 cm [3 inches] in k2, p2 rib for waistband. Change to 1.75 mm (2) hook 2 ch and work 1 tr in each of the k sts, 2 turning ch.

NOTE.— The Contrast spots are worked in every other row and have 9 Main colour stitches between each spot. Each spot is worked in the 5th of the 9 Main colour sts which were worked between each of the spots of the last spotted row.

Working in tr and keeping the spot pattern constant, work 1 edge straight for the centre front but at the side edge * work 1 row, inc once in the next row *. Work from * to * 9 times more. Work on without further shaping until the front measures 26.5 cm [10½ inches]

This charming spotted cardigan features a neat collar

or the desired underarm seam measurement ending at armhole edge and right side facing.
SHAPE ARMHOLE.—Sl.st over 6 sts, work to end.
Next row: work to last 4 sts, turn.
Next row: sl.st over 3 sts, work to end.
Next row: work to last 3 sts, turn.
Next row: sl.st over 3 sts, work to end.
On next 4 rows dec 1 st at armhole edge. (73 sts).
Cont straight until work measures 12.5 cm [5 inches] from beg of armhole ending at centre front edge.
SHAPE NECK.—Sl.st across 12 sts, work to end.
Next row: work to last 6 sts, turn.
Next row: sl.st over 4 sts, work to end.
Next row: work to last 3 sts, turn.
Next row: sl.st over 2 sts, work to end.
Next row: work to last 2 sts, tr 2tog, turn.
Next row: tr 2tog, work to end. (45 sts).
SHAPE SHOULDER.—Sl.st across 5 sts, work to end. Cont dec 5 sts at side edge every row until all sts are cast off.
Fasten off.

RIGHT FRONT.—Work as for Left Front reversing all shapings.

BACK.—With 2¼mm (13) needles and M, cast on 126 sts and k into back of sts. Work 7.5 cm

[3 inches] in k2, p2 rib. Change to crochet and pattern as for Left Front.
* Work 1 row. Increase once at the beg and end of the next row*. Work from * to * 9 times more.
When work measures same as fronts to armholes, shape armhole.
SHAPE ARMHOLES.—Dec 2 sts at each end of work for 5 rows and then dec 1 st at each end of work until 112 sts rem.
When armholes measure the same as those for fronts, dec 5 sts at each end of every row for the next 7 rows.
Fasten off.

SLEEVES.—With 1.75 mm (2) hook and M, ch 92 and work a dc in each ch to end of row. Change to pattern and work straight for 4 rows. Inc 1 st at beg and end of next 7 foll alt rows.
SHAPE TOP.—Dec 6 sts at beg and end of next row.
Next row: dec 4 sts at beg and end of next row.
Next 2 rows: dec 3 sts at beg and end of row.
Dec 2 sts at beg and end of every row until 23 sts rem.
Fasten off.

COLLAR.—With 1.75 mm (2) hook and M, ch 127 and work in pattern for 15 rows without shaping.
Fasten off.

TO MAKE UP.—With right sides together overstitch side and shoulder seams; also the underarm seams of sleeve. Carefully ease sleeve into armhole matching seams and centre of sleeve with shoulder seam. Stitch carefully. Ease collar on to neck edge with wrong side of collar to right side of garment. To neaten edge of collar, work 2 rows of dc round all three sides of collar, working (1 dc, 1 ch, 1 dc) at each corner.

FRONT BORDERS.—With 1.75 mm (2) hook and M, work 5 rows in stitch 3 down edges of fronts making 5 buttonholes in Right Front border. Mark positions for buttons on Left Front border and work buttonholes to correspond in the 2nd row of dc by working 5 ch over 5 dc for each. In next row work 1 dc in each ch.
See ball band for pressing instructions.

STRIPED COTTON SWEATER

1 9 3 9

* Lightweight nubbly cotton yarn is used for an easy-fitting jumper worked from side to side with contrast stripes and collar. The yoke and sleeves are worked in the usual way

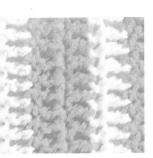

MATERIALS.—Rowan Salad Days Cotton: 6(7:8) 50 g balls Main colour; 2(2:2) 50 g balls Contrast colour; 2.50 mm (2) crochet hook; pair of 2¾ mm (12) knitting needles; 4 buttons.
TENSION.—5 sts and 3 rows over 2.5 cm [1 inch] of stitch 1.
STITCHES.—1. trebles; 2. double crochet; 3. k1, p1 rib.
SIZES.—To fit bust 86(91:97) cm [34(36:38) inches]. Actual measurement: 94(99:104) cm [37(39:41) inches]; length 58.5 cm [23 inches]; sleeve seam 11.5 cm [4½ inches].
Figures in brackets () refer to larger sizes.
ABBREVIATIONS.—C-Contrast colour; ch-chain; cont-continue; dc-double crochet; dec-decrease; inc-increase; M-Main colour; sl.st-slip stitch; st(s)-stitch(es); tog-together; tr-treble; yrh-yarn round hook

FRONT.—With 2.50 hook and M, make 66 ch, yrh, hook in 3rd ch from hook and work 1 tr in this and all subsequent ch to end of row, 2 turning ch. 64 sts.
Work 1 tr row with M then 1 tr row with C ending with 5 ch. The colour sequence is 2 rows M, 1 row C.
SHAPE ARMHOLE.—1 tr in 3rd ch from hook, 1 tr in each next 2 ch, cont in tr to end, 2 turning ch.
next row: work in tr to end, 4 turning ch.
next row: 1 tr in 3rd ch, 1 tr in next ch, work in tr to end, 2 turning ch.
Continue inc 2 sts at armhole edge every row until there are 79 sts. Continue straight in pattern until there are 15(17:19) white stripes. Work 2 rows.
Dec 2 sts at armhole edge of next 6 rows.
Dec 3 sts on next row.
(Work should end with 2 yellow rows.) **.
Fasten off.

FRONT YOKE.—With 2.50 mm (2) hook and M work 65(75:85) tr across top of front. Work 9 rows in tr.
SHAPE NECK.—Work 26(31:36) tr.
next row, sl.st across 3 sts, work to end.
next row: work to last 2 sts, turn.
next row: dec 2 tog, work to end.
next row: work to last 2 sts, dec 2tog.
next row: dec 2 tog, work to end.18(23:13) sts.
SHAPE SHOULDER.—Sl.st across 8(11:13) sts at armhole edge, 1 dc in next st, work in tr to end.
next row: work to last 2 tr, dec 2tog, sl.st to next st of previous row.
Fasten off.
Leave centre 13 sts unworked and complete second side to match first, reversing shapings.

BACK.—Work as for Front to **.

BACK YOKE. - With 2.50 mm (2) hook and M, work 65(75:85) tr across top of Back. Work 1 row.
next row: work 33(38:43) tr. Turn and work

this side 10 rows with 4 buttonholes.
Sl.st across 11 sts from centre of work. Work
to end. Work to last 3 sts, dec 3tog, turn, dec
3tog, work to end.
SHAPE SHOULDER.—Work as for Front.
Complete second side to match, making 4
more tr to form 4 st underlap and sl.st across
14 sts from centre of work.

COLLAR.—(make 2) Sew shoulder seams.
With 2.50 mm (2) hook and C work a row of dc
round neck from back to centre front leaving
underlap sts unworked. Continue in dc until
work measures 7 cm [2 inches], inc 1 st at
centre front edge every second row.

SLEEVES.—With 2.50 mm (2) hook and M,
make 71 ch, yrh, hook in 2nd ch from hook
and work 1 dc in this and all subsequent ch to
end of row, 1 turning ch. 70 sts. Work 5 rows in
dc ending with 2 turning ch.
Change to tr and inc 1 st at beg of next 6 rows.
76 sts. Work 6 rows.
SHAPE ARMHOLE.—Sl.st across 15 sts,
work to last 15 sts, turn.
Dec 2tog at each end of next 16 rows.
Fasten off.

WELTS.—With 2¾ mm (12) needles and M,
pick up and k 100(112:124) sts along base of
Back. Work in k1, p1 rib for 5 cm [2 inches].
Cast off ribwise.
Work similar rib along base of Front.

TO MAKE UP.—Sew shoulder, side and
sleeve seams. Set sleeves into armholes.
Secure underlap. Sew on buttons.
See ball band for pressing instructions.

casual wear

ZIPPER JACKET

** Originally knitted in a basket weave stitch, this
zipper jacket has been re-worked in relief trebles to
give a similar look. A neat tie adds the finishing touch
with a bow at the neck

MATERIALS.—Rowan 4 ply wool:
22(25:28:31) 25 g hanks balls; 4 mm (8)
crochet hook; pair of 3¼ mm (10) knitting
needles; lightweight zip fastener 43 cm [17
inches].
TENSION.—7 sts to 2.5 cm [1 inch]; 8 rows
to 5 cm [2 inches] over pattern.
STITCHES.—1. relief front and back trebles;
2. k2, p2 rib; 3. stocking stitch.
SIZES.—To fit bust 86(91:97:102) cm
[34(36:38:40) inches]. Actual measurements:
97(102:107:112) cm [38(40:42:44) inches];
length 62.5(64:64:65) cm [24½(25:25:25½)
inches]; sleeve seam 46 cm [18 inches].
Figures in brackets () refer to larger sizes.
ABBREVIATIONS.—ch-chain; dc-double
crochet; inc-increase k-knit; p-purl; rb/tr-
yarn round hook, put hook from behind and
from right to left round stem of stitch and
complete in usual way; rep-repeat; rf/tr-yarn
round hook, put hook from in front and from
right to left round stem of stitch and complete
in usual way; sl.st-slip stitch; st.st-stocking
st; tr-treble.

BACK.—With 3¼ mm (10) needles cast on
122(130:138:146) sts and work in k2, p2 rib
for 13 cm [5 inches] using a larger needle for
last rib row. Change to 4 mm (8) hook and
work 2 ch in first st then 1 tr in each next st of
rib to end of work, 2 turning ch.
row 1: miss first tr, * 1 rf/tr in each next 4 tr, 1
rb/tr in each next 4 tr; rep from * ending with
1 tr in turning ch, 2 turning ch.
rows 2-4: as row 1.
row 5: miss first st, * 1 rb/tr in each next 4 sts,
1 rf/tr in each next 4 sts; rep from * ending
with 1 tr in turning ch, 2 turning ch.
rows 6-8: as row 5
These 8 rows form pattern.
Keeping in pattern, inc 1 st at either edge on
next and every following 4th row until there
are 134(140:148:154) sts. Continue until work
measures 41 cm [16 inches].
SHAPE ARMHOLE.—Sl.st across 7 sts,
work to last 7 sts, turn.
Dec 1 st at each end of next 6 rows.
Continue straight until armhole measures
21.5(23:23:24) cm [8½(9:9:9½) inches] working
the last row to the last 33(36:38:41) sts, then
turn, work next 42(42:46:46) sts.
Fasten off.

FRONT.—Work as for Back until last row of
rib is completed. With 4 mm (8) hook, 2 ch in
first st, work 1 tr in next 59(63:67:71) sts, turn
and continue on this side. Keeping in pattern
work 8 rows then on next and every following
4th row, inc 1 st at side edge until there are
66(69:73:76) sts.
Continue until work measures same as Back
to armhole, ending at armhole edge.
SHAPE ARMHOLE.—Sl.st across 7 sts,
work to end.
Dec 1 st at armhole edge on next 6 rows.

A bow tied at the collar gives this useful jacket a note of femininity

Continue straight until work measures 15 cm [6 inches] ending at neck edge.
SHAPE NECK.—Sl.st across 4(4:6:6:) sts at neck edge, work to end.
On next and following 3 rows, dec 4 sts at neck edge. 33(36:38:41) sts.
Continue straight until armhole measures same for Back.
Fasten off.
Rejoin yarn to other part of Front, sl.st across 2 sts at centre edge. Work as for first Front reversing all shapings.
Work 1 row of dc all round the centre opening and round neck edge to neaten.

SLEEVES.—With 3¼ mm (10) needles, cast on 64(64:72:72) sts and work in k2, p2 rib for 10 cm [4 inches] using a larger needle for last row of rib. Change to 4 mm (8) hook, work 2 ch in first st then 1 tr in each rib st, 2 turning ch. Continue in pattern inc 1 st either side of next row then every 8th row until there are 84(86:88:90) sts, incorporatng the new sts into the pattern.

Work until sleeve measures 46 cm [18 inches].
SHAPE TOP.—Sl.st across 7 sts, work to last 7 sts, turn.
Dec 1 st at beg of every row until 26 sts remain.
Fasten off.

COLLAR.—With 4 mm (8) hook make 19 ch, hook into 3rd ch from hook and work 1 tr in this and all subsequent ch to end of row, 2 turning ch.
next row: miss first st, (4 rf/tr, 4 rb/tr) twice, 1 tr in turning ch.
Continue in pattern as set reversing the pattern after every 4 rows until collar fits nicely round the neck. Work 1 row of dc round collar edge to neaten.
Fasten off.

TIE.—With 3¼ mm (10) needles, cast on 2 sts. Work in st.st inc 1 st in each row at same one side only to form a point until work measures 5 cm [2 inches]. When 15 rows have been worked for the beginning, change to reverse stocking st and work a further 15 rows. Continue working in blocks of 15 rows until work measures 102 cm [40 inches] approximately. (The work needs to be long enough to go under the collar and then tie in a neat bow.)
Then shape the 2nd point by k2 tog at the front in every row at one side only until 2 sts rem.
Cast off.

TO MAKE UP.—Sew side and sleeve seams. Sew sleeves to armholes, sew collar to neck. With 3¼ mm (10) needles work 2 strips of st.st 8 sts wide and approximately 43 cm [17 inches] long to fit centre front opening when slightly stretched.
Sew the zip fastener in position, facing either side with the two strips of st.st.
See ball band for pressing instructions.

STRIPED SWEATER

1953

* This V-necked sweater, boldly striped in two colours, is worked in simple trebles. The V-neck, cuffs and welts are knitted in rib in the main colour for additional emphasis

MATERIALS.—Pingouin France: 6(7:8:9: 10) 50 g balls Main colour; 3(3:4:4:5) 50 g balls Contrast colour; 4 mm (8) crochet hook; pair of 3¼ mm (10) knitting needles.

TENSION.—17 sts and 10 rows to 10 cm [4 inches] over trebles.

STITCHES.—1. trebles; 2. k1, p1.

SIZES.—To fit chest 91(97:102:107:112) cm [36(38:40:42:44) inches]. Actual measurements 97(102:107:112:117) cm [38(40:42:44: 46) inches]; length from shoulder 56(56:56: 58.5:58.5) cm [22(22:22:23:23) inches]; sleeve seam 47 cm [18½ inches].

Figures in brackets () refer to larger sizes.

ABBREVIATIONS.—alt-alternate; beg-beginning; C-contrast; ch-chain; cont-continue; dec-decrease; foll-following; inc-increase k-knit; M-main; p-purl; rem-remaining; rep-repeat; sl.st-slip stitch; st(s)-stitch(es); tr-treble; yrh-yarn round hook.

NOTE.—1. When changing from one colour to another colour, drop old colour and pick up new colour before you complete your last st in old colour so that the loop on the hook afterwards is already in the new colour. Make sure colour not in use is put to front of work before you change colour so that yarn is at back of work in next row.

2. To decrease over trebles, work 2 sts as follows: yrh, hook into first stitch, yrh, draw through a loop, yrh, draw through 2 loops, yrh, hook into next st, yrh, draw through a loop, yrh, draw through 2 loops, yrh, draw through 3 loops (1 dec worked).

3. To increase over trebles, work twice into stitch.

BACK.— With 4 mm (8) hook and M make 84(88:92:96:100) ch.

next row: Using M, miss 2 ch (counts as 1 tr) and work 1 tr in each next 5(7:9:11:13) ch, [6(8:10:12:14] tr worked. Change to C and work 1 tr in each next 18 ch, with M, work 1 tr in each next 34 ch, in C work 1 tr in each next 18 ch, with M work 1 tr in each next 6(8:10:12:14) ch, 2 turning ch.

Rep this row but working into tr from previous row and keeping C panels correct until work measures 56(56:56:58.5:58.5) cm [22(22:22:23:23) inches], ending with right side facing.

SHAPE SHOULDERS.—Sl.st across first 12(13:14:15:16) sts, patt to last 12(13:14:15: 16) sts, turn, sl.st across first 12(13:14:15:16) sts, patt to last 12(13:14:15:16) sts.

Fasten off.

FRONT.—Work as for Back until the work measures 31(31:31:33.5:33.5) cm [12¼(12¼:12¼: 13¼:13¼) inches] ending with the right side of the work facing.

SHAPE V-NECK.—Keeping pattern and colour panels correct, work 41(43:45:47:49) sts and turn. Work on these sts for first side, dec 1 st at neck edge on every row until 24(26:28:30:32) sts rem. Cont in patt until work measures same as Back to shoulder ending with right side facing.

SHAPE SHOULDERS.—Sl.st across 12(13: 14:15:16) sts, pattern to end.

Fasten off.

Rejoin yarns to rem sts and complete to match first side.

SLEEVES.—With 4 mm (8) hook and M make 46 ch and work in patt as on Body setting trebles as follows: 13M, 18C, 13M.

Now at the same time and keeping patt correct, inc sts worked in M. Inc 1 st at each end of every row until there are 56 sts, then each end of every alt row until there are 84 sts. Cont in patt until work measures 39.5 cm [15½ inches].

Fasten off.

WELTS.—(worked separately) With 3¼ mm (10) needles, M and right side facing, pick up and k 82(86:90:94:98) sts evenly along base ch. Dec 6 sts evenly across first row working in k1, p1 rib for 7.5 cm [3 inches].

Cast off ribwise allowing for natural ease.

CUFFS.—With 3¼ mm (10) needles, M and right side facing, pick up and k 44 sts along base ch and work in k1, p1 rib for 7.5 [3 inches].

Cast off ribwise allowing for natural ease.

NECKBAND.—Join right shoulder seam. With 3¼ mm (10) needles, M and right side facing, pick up and k approx 50 sts down left front neck, 1 st at centre front, 50 sts up right front neck, 34 sts across back neck and work in k1, p1 rib for 6 rows, dec 1 st each side of centre front st on every row.

Cast off ribwise, dec 1 st each side of centre front stitch as before.

TO MAKE UP.—Join left shoulder and neck-band seams. Set sleeves in place, with centre of sleeve to shoulder seam and the rest set evenly each side, sew into place. Sew in all ends from colour panels. Sew side and sleeve seams.

See ball band for pressing instructions.

OPENWORK JUMPER

AND TOPS

1 9 6 7

* Lightweight sweater with scoop-neck worked straight for an easy fit in a fluffy yarn and a puff stitch with double crochet trim. The sleeves are worked directly on to the sweater

MATERIALS.—Phildar Phil'Soft: 9(9:10) 50 g balls; 4.50 mm (7) crochet hook.

TENSION.—5 puff sts to 5 cm [2 inches]), 8 rows to 7 cm [2¾ inches].

STITCHES.—1. puff stitch; 2: double crochet.

SIZES.—To fit bust 86(91:97) cm [34(36:38) inches]. Actual measurements: 94(99:104) cm [37(39:41) inches]; length 62(63.5:64.5) cm [24½(25:25½) inches: sleeve seam 43 cm [17 inches].

NOTE: Jumper is shorter than original.

Figures in brackets () refer to larger sizes.
ABBREVIATIONS.—beg-beginning; ch-chain; dc-double crochet; rep-repeat; st(s)-stitch(es); tr-treble; yrh-yarn round hook

BACK.—With 4.50 mm (7), make a loose ch of 97(103:107) yrh, work 1 tr in 2nd ch from hook, * yrh and draw up a look in next ch, yrh, draw up a loop in next ch (5 loops on hook), yrh and draw through all loops (1 puff stitch made), 1 ch to fasten; rep from * to end ending with 1 tr in last ch, 2 turning ch. This is the foundation row.
row 1: 1 tr in tr, yrh, draw up a loop between this and next puff st, yrh and draw up a loop in same space, yrh and draw through all 5 loops, 1 ch to fasten, * yrh, draw up a loop in space between next 2 puff sts, yrh and draw up another loop in same space, yrh and draw through all 5 loops, 1 ch to fasten; rep from * omitting the 1 ch fastening for last puff st and ending with 1 tr in turning ch, 2 turning ch. This row forms pattern.
Continue in patt until work measures 43 cm [17 inches] from beg or desired length to armholes.
Place a marker at this point.
Work straight until work measures 19(20.5: 21.5) cm [7½(8:8½) inches] from marker.
SHAPE NECK AND SHOULDERS.—Work 15(16:17) puff sts.
Fasten off.
Rejoin yarn to beg of last 15(16:17) sts and work to end.

FRONT.—Work as for Back until work measures 9(10:11.5) cm [3½(4:4½) inches] from armhole marker.
SHAPE NECK.—Work across 18(19:20) puff sts ending at neck edge, 1 turning ch.
At neck edge, dec 2 puff sts together on next three rows. Work straight until work measures same as Back to shoulder.
Fasten off.
Rejoin yarn to beg of last 18(19:20) puff sts

and work to correspond with other side. Sew shoulder seams.

SLEEVES.—Starting at one armhole marker join in yarn on previous row, 2 ch, patt 39(41:43) puff sts along armhole to second marker working a tr in st at end of row. Work 4 rows ending with 1 tr in turning ch. Dec 2 puff sts together at the beg and end of next row then every 3rd row until there are 15(17:19) puff sts. Work straight until sleeve is 43 cm [17 inches] or desired length to wrist. Loosely work 1 row of slip stitch. Fasten off.

TO MAKE UP.—Sew side and sleeve seams. Work 3 rows of dc round neck edge allowing for stretch to fit over the head. Fasten off. See ball band for pressing instructions.

JACKET WITH SPOTS

1 9 6 6

** *Close-fitting, long sleeved cardigan jacket worked in firm double crochet with a spot pattern in a contrast colour which is also used to trim the edge of the jacket*

MATERIALS.—Robin Colombine Crepe DK: 9(10:10) 50 g balls Main colour; 1(2:2) 50 g balls Contrast colour; 4.50 mm (7) crochet hook; 6 buttons.

TENSION.—16 sts and 17 rows to 10 cm [4 inches] over stitch 2.

STITCHES.—1. double crochet; 2. bobble stitch.

SIZES.—To fit bust 81(86:91) cm [32(34:36) inches]. Actual measurements 88(93:98) cm [34½(36½:38½ inches]; length from centre back neck 59(62:64) cm [23¼(24½:25¼) inches]; sleeve seam 46(47:48) cm [18(18½:19) inches]. Figures in brackets () refer to larger sizes.

ABBREVIATIONS.—alt-alternate; b1-make bobble (1 ch,[yrh, hook through next st and draw through a loop] 4 times, yarn through all 9 loops on hook); beg-beginning; C-contrast colour; ch-chain; cont-continue; dc-double crochet; dec-decrease; foll-following; M-main colour; patt-pattern; rem-remaining; rep-repeat; st(s)-stitch(es); tog-together; yrh-yarn round hook.

BACK.—With 4.50 mm (7) hook and M ch 68(72:76) loosely, yrh, put hook into 2nd ch from hook and work 1 dc in this and all subsequent ch to end of work. 67(71:75) sts. This is the foundation row. Now work in pattern.

row 1: (wrong side) 1 ch (this counts as first st), miss first st, 1 dc in each st to end of row (working last dc in turning ch. (67:71:75 sts). Rep this row twice more.

NOTE: Use a separate length of C for each bobble.

row 4: (right side) 1 ch, 1 dc in each of next 0(2:4) sts, * using C, b1, using M, 1 ch, 1 dc in (each next 15 sts; repeat from * to last 2(4:6) sts, using C, b1, using M, 1 ch, 1 dc in each st to end of row, 1 turning ch.

row 5: 1 dc in each st to end of row working dcs across b1 of previous rows through single M loop across back, 1 turning ch.

Rep row 1 twelve times more.

row 18: 1 ch, 1 dc in each next 1(3:5) sts, * 1 dc in each next 7 sts, using C, b1, using M, 1 ch, 1 dc into each of next 8 sts; rep from * to last 2(4:6) sts, 1 dc in each st to end.

row 19: as row 5.

Rep row 1 nine times more.

These 28 rows form patt and are repeated throughout.

Cont straight until work measures 38(39:40) cm [15(15½:15¾) inches] ending after a wrong side row.

SHAPE RAGLAN.—Sl.st across 5 sts, 1 ch to count as first st, work to last 5 sts, turn. 57(61:65) sts.

Co-ordinating spots and jacket trim contrast pleasingly with the main colour

Work one row in pattern.

Dec2 tog at both ends of next and every foll alt row 13(14:15) times in all. 31(33:35) sts.

Work one row in pattern.

SHAPE NECK.—Next row: (right side) patt across first 8 sts then dec2 tog at beg of next row and turn. 7 sts remain.

Work on these 7 sts only for first side.

** Work 6 rows in pattern, dec2 tog at neck edge of first 2 rows and dec2 tog at raglan edge of 2nd and every foll alt row. 2 sts remain.

Work these 2 sts tog.

Fasten off.

Return to rem 23(25:27) sts. Miss centre 15(17:19) sts and rejoin yarn to next st with right side facing, 1 ch, pattern to last 2 sts, dec2 tog. 7 sts remain.

Complete second side to match first from **.

LEFT FRONT.—With 4.50 mm (7) hook and M, ch 36(38:40) loosely. Work foundation row as given for Back. 35(37:39) sts.

Now work in patt as given for Back, positioning patt thus:

row 4: (right side) 1 ch, 1 dc in each next 0(2:4) sts, * using C, b1, using M, 1 ch, 1 dc in each next 15 sts; rep from * to last 2 sts, using C, b1, using M, 1 dc in last st, turn.

Cont straight until Front measures same as Back to raglan shaping ending after same patt row.

SHAPE RAGLAN.—Sl.st across 5 sts at beg of next row. (For Right Front, work to last 5 sts, turn.) 30(32:34) sts.

Work one row in pattern.

Dec2 tog at raglan edge of next and every foll alt row 11(12:13) times in all. 19(20:21) sts.

Work one row in pattern.

SHAPE NECK.—Dec 2 tog at raglan edge, work to last 9(10:11) sts at neck edge, turn.

Work 10 rows in patt, dec2 tog at neck edge of first 2 rows and at raglan edge of 2nd and

every foll alt row. 2 sts remain. Work these 2 sts tog.

Fasten off.

RIGHT FRONT.—Work as given for Left Front, noting the bracketed exception and positioning pattern thus:

row 4: (right side) 1 ch, * using C, b1, using M, 1 ch, 1 dc in each next 15 sts; rep from * to last 2(4:6) sts, using C, b1, using M, 1 ch, 1 dc in each st to end, turn.

SLEEVES.—With 4.50 mm (7) hook and M, ch 36(38:40) loosely.

Work foundation row as given for Back. 35(37:39) sts.

Now work in patt as given for Back, positioning patt thus:

row 4: (right side) 1 ch, 1 dc in each next 0(1:2) sts, * using C, b1, using M, 1 ch, 1 dc in each next 15 sts; rep from * to last 2(3:4) sts, using C, b1, using M, 1 ch, 1 dc in each st to end.

Inc 1 st (make inc by working 2 dc in second or last but one st) at both ends of 7th and every foll 4th row 9 times in all. 53(55:57) sts.

Cont straight until work measures 46(47:48) cm [18(18½:19) inches] ending after same number of rows since b1 row as on Back.

SHAPE RAGLAN.—Sl.st across 5 sts, work to last 5 sts, turn.

Work 1 row in pattern. Dec2 tog at both ends of next and every foll alt row until 7(9:9) sts remain.

Work one row in pattern.

Fasten off.

TO MAKE UP.—Join raglan seams. Join side and sleeve seams. Mark positions of 6 buttonholes along Right Front opening edge: top buttonhole to be 1 cm [½ inch] below neck edge, bottom buttonhole to be 2.5 cm [1 inch] above lower edge and remaining four evenly spaced between.

With 4.50 mm (7) hook, M and right side facing, work 1 row dc along front opening and neck edges working 2 sts into neck corners.

Fasten off.

With 4.50 mm (7) hook, C and right side facing, re-join yarn at right side seam lower edge and work 1 row dc around entire front opening, neck and hem edge, working 2 sts into corners and making buttonholes at positions marked thus:

2 ch, miss 2 sts.

Work a further 3 rows in dc making 2 dc in each ch space using C.

Fasten off.

Sew on buttons.

See ball band for pressing instructions.

BASKET STITCH SWEATER

1 9 8 3

*** A simple, unisex, long sleeved, V-necked sweater is worked in a basket stitch pattern using alternating relief trebles. Knitted ribs form the cuffs, welts and neck edging*

MATERIALS.—Rowan 4 ply wool: 22(25: 28:31:34:37) 25 g hanks; 3.50 mm (9) crochet hook; pair of 2¾ mm (12) knitting needles.
TENSION. 28 sts and 20 rows to 10 cm [4 inches] over stitch 1 slightly stretched.
STITCHES.—1. basket pattern; 2. k1, p1 rib.
SIZES.—To fit bust/chest 86(91:97:102:107: 112) cm 34(36:38:40:42:44) inches]. Actual measurements: 91(97:102:107:112:117) cm [36(38:40:42:44:46) inches]; length at shoulder 70(70:71:72.5:74:74) cm [27½(27½:28: 28½:29:29) inches]; sleeve seam 51 cm [20 inches].

Figures in brackets () refer to larger sizes.
ABBREVIATIONS.—ch-chain; cont-continue; dec-decrease; inc-increase; k-knit; p-purl; patt-pattern; rb/tr-yarn round hook, hook in from back and from right to left round stem of stitch and complete in usual way; rem-remaining; rep-repeat; rf/tr-yarn round hook, hook from front and right to left round stem of st and complete in usual way; sl.-slip; st(s)-stitch(es); tr-treble; yrh-yarn round hook.

BACK.—With 3.50 mm (9) hook make 123(131:135:143:147:155), yrh, hook in 3rd ch from hook and work a tr in this and all subsequent ch to end, 2 turning ch. 121(129:133:141:145:153) sts.
This is the foundation row.
row 1: miss first st, * 1 rf.tr in each next 4 sts, 1 rb/tr in each next 4 sts; rep from * ending with 1 tr in turning ch, 2 turning ch.
row 2: as row 1.
row 3: as row 1.
row 4: as row 1.
row 5: miss first st, * 1 rb/tr in each next 4 sts, 1 rf/tr in each next 4 sts; rep from * ending with 1 tr in turning ch, 2 turning ch.
row 6: as row 5.
row 7: as row 5.
row 8: as row 5.
These 8 rows form pattern.
Cont in patt inc 1 st at each end of next row then every foll 8th row until there are 129(137:141:149:153:161) sts incorporating extra sts into patt. Cont straight until work measures 43 cm [17 inches].
SHAPE ARMHOLES.—Sl.st across 6(7:7:8: 8:9) sts, work in patt to last 6(7:7:8:8:9) sts, turn. **
Dec 1 st at each end of next 3 rows then every 4th row until 99(105:111:117:119:123) sts remain.
Cont without shaping until work measures 19(19:20.5:21.5:23:23) cm [7½(7½:8:8½:9:9) inches] from armhole shaping.

Ribbed neck edging gives definition to the basket stitch pattern of this V-neck sweater

SHAPE SHOULDERS.—Sl.st across 10(11:11:11:12:12) sts, work to last 10(11:11:11:12:12) sts, turn.

next row: sl.st across 10(11:11:11:12:12:12) sts, work to last 10(11:11:12:12:12) sts.

next row: sl.st across 11(11:12:12:12:13) sts, work to last 11(11:12:12:12:13) sts, turn.

Fasten off.

With 2¾ mm (12) needles, pick up and k 115(123:131:139:147:155) sts from base of work. Work in k1, p1 rib until work measures 7.5 cm [3 inches]. Cast off ribwise.

FRONT.—Work as for Back to **.

Dec 1 st at each end of next 2 rows.

SHAPE V-NECK.—Dec 1 st at armhole edge, patt 56(59:61:64:66:69) sts, turn. Cont on this group.

Dec 1 st at armhole and at neck edge on next and every row until there are 50(53:54:59:60:62) sts. Cont dec at neck edge only on every row until 40(43:44:49:50:52) sts rem then on every 8th row until 31(33:34:35:36:37) sts rem.

Cont straight until Front measures same as Back to shoulder shaping, ending at armhole edge.

SHAPE SHOULDER.—Sl.st across 10(11:11:11:12:12) sts, work to end, turn. Work to last 10(11:11:11:12:13) sts, turn and work rem sts.

Fasten off.

Rejoin yarn to second side and work to match first side leaving centre st unworked.

Work rib as given for Back.

SLEEVES.—With 3.50 mm (9) hook make 63(67:71:71:79:79) ch, yrh, hook in 3rd ch from hook and work 1 tr in this and all subsequent ch to end of row, 2 turning ch. 60(64:68:68:76:76) sts.

Cont in patt as for Back, inc 1 st at each end of 9th then every following 3rd row until there are 92(92:98:106:112:118) sts then on every following 4th row until there are 98(104:110:116:122:128) sts incorporating extra sts into patt.

Continue straight until work measures approximately 43 cm 17 inches ending after similar patt row as on Back before armhole shaping.

SHAPE TOP.—Sl.st across first 6(7:7:8:8:9) sts, patt to last 6(7:7:8:8:9) sts, turn.

Work 2 rows straight.

Dec 1 st at each end of every row until 44 sts remain then 2 sts at each end of every row until 32 sts remain.

Fasten off.

With 2¾ mm (12) knitting needles, pick up and k approximately 57(59:61:63:65:67) sts and work in k1, p1 rib until rib measures 7.5 cm [3 inches)]

Cast off ribwise.

NECKBAND.—Join shoulder seams.

With 2¾ mm (12) needles cast on 2 sts and work as follows:

row 1: p2.

row 2: (k1, p1) in first st, (p1, k1) in next st.

row 3: p1, k2, p1.

row 4: k1, (p1, k1) in next st, (k1, p1) in next st, k1.

row 5: p1, k1, p2, k1, p1.

row 6: k1, p1, (k1, p1) in next st, (p1, k1) in next st, p1, k1.

Cont in this way working 2 sts into each of the two centre sts of every even numbered row until there are 24 sts.

next row: rib.

next row: rib 12, turn and leave rem sts on stitch holder. Cont on these 12 sts until strip fits up front edge and round to centre back of neck, allowing for the rib to be a little stretched.

Cast off in rib.

Rejoin yarn to rem sts and work 2nd strip to match first.

TO MAKE UP.—Sew neckband in position and join at centre back neck with a flat seam. Set sleeves into place, easing to fit, sew in neatly. Sew side and sleeve seams.

See ball band for pressing instructions.

S CARF-COLLARED JUMPER

1 9 3 2

*** *Two separately worked scarves in two colours twist loosely round the neck of this jumper worked in star stitch on a Tunisian crochet hook and with rib knit cuffs and welts*

MATERIALS.—Phildar Luxe: 6(7) 50 g balls Main colour; 1(1) 50 g ball Contrast colour; 4 mm (8) Tunisian crochet hook; pair of 2 mm (14) knitting needles; a 3¾ mm (9) knitting needle.

TENSION.—5 patterns to 5.5 cm [2¼ inches] approximately.

STITCHES.—1. k1, p1 rib; 2. star pattern.

SIZES.—To fit bust 81(86) cm [32(34) inches]. Actual measurement: 86(91) cm [34(36) inches]; length to shoulder 42 cm [16½ inches]; sleeve seam 46 cm [18 inches].

Figures in brackets () refer to larger sizes.

ABBREVIATIONS.—ch-chain; cont-continue; C-Contrast colour; dec-decrease; inc-increase; k-knit; M-Main colour; p-purl; rep-repeat; st(s)-stitch(es); yrh-yarn round hook.

FRONT.—With 2 mm (14) needles and M (used double), cast on 109(115) sts and work in k1, p1 rib for 7.5 cm [3 inches] changing to a 3¾ mm (9) needle for last row and dec evenly along row to 98(104) sts.

Change to crochet pattern and single yarn. NOTE Tunisian crochet is worked over an outward and a return row and these 2 rows are counted as one row in the instructions.

Put all sts on to 4 mm (8) Tunisian hook.

Foundation row 1: (return) yrh, draw loop through first st, * yrh, draw loop through 2 sts; rep from * to end, 1 turning ch.

pattern row 1: (outward) * hook through first 3 loops from right to left, yrh, draw loop through, 1 ch, 1 loop through each next 2 horizontal sts (made visible by the drawing together of first 3 vertical sts); rep from * to end of row. There should be the same number of loops on hook as on Foundation row.

pattern row: (return) yrh, draw loop through first st, * yrh, draw loop through 2 sts; rep from * to end, 1 turning ch.

Work in pattern for 4 cm [1½ inches] then inc 1 st at each end every 2 rows until there are 106(112) sts and at the same time when crochet pattern measures 20 cm [8 inches] divide for neck.

Work first side still increasing 1 st every 2 rows at the side edge and leaving 1 st every 2 rows at neck edge. When pattern measures 25 cm [10 inches], shape armhole.

SHAPE ARMHOLE.—Leave 6 sts at each armhole edge on first row and 2 sts in each next 2 rows. **For second size only:** dec 1 st more either side of next row. Work armhole edge straight but cont neck dec until there are 36 sts and then work straight until armhole measures 15 cm [6 inches].

SHAPE SHOULDER.—Dec 9 sts at armhole edge until all sts have been absorbed. Fasten off.

Work second side to match.

BACK.—Work as for Front omitting neck

shaping. Shape armhole when there are 118(124) sts and work measures 25.5 cm [10 inches]. When work is 41 cm [16 inches], leave 26(32) centre sts for neck.
Work first and second sides as for Front.

SLEEVES.—With 2 mm (14) needles and single yarn cast on 70 sts and work in k1, p1 rib for 16 cm [6¼ inches] and dec 8 sts evenly along last row using larger size needle. Change to 4 mm (8) hook and work 8 rows in crochet pattern. Cont, inc 1 st at each side of work every 6th row until there are 74 sts and sleeve measures 46 cm [18 inches].
SHAPE TOP.—Leave 3 sts at each side of work on each row until 20 sts are left.

Fasten off.

SCARVES.—(work 1 in M, 1 in C). With 4 mm (8) hook, make 3 ch and work in pattern. Inc 1 st in each row at one side of work until there are 18 sts. Work for 91 cm [36 inches], then dec 1 st in each row at one side of work until 3 sts are left.
Fasten off.

TO MAKE UP—Block each piece of work to shape. Sew shoulder seams. Sew sleeves to armholes, sew side and sleeve seams. Twist the two scarf lengths together loosely and sew to edge of neck leaving ends free.
See ball band for pressing instructions.

STRIPED CREW-NECK JUMPER

1 9 3 2

*** *This jumper is worked in an unusual chevron stitch using a Tunisian crochet hook. The deep cuffs and welts are knitted in a fine rib, and rib edges the crew neck*

MATERIALS.—Rowan 4 ply Botany wool: 7 25 g hanks Main colour; 4 25 g hanks colour A; 3 25 g hanks colour B; 4 mm (8) Tunisian crochet hook; pair of 2¾ mm (12) knitting needles; set of four 2¾ mm (12) double pointed needles; one 3¾ mm (9) knitting needle.

TENSION.—1 pattern (6 sts) to 2.5 cm [1 inch] approximately over 4 mm (8) Tunisian hook.

STITCHES.—1. k1, p1 rib; 2. chevron pattern.

SIZES.—To fit bust 81(86) cm [32(34) inches]. Actual measurement: 89(94) cm [35(37) inches]; length 44.5 cm [17½ inches]; sleeve seam 44.5 cm [17½ inches].

ABBREVIATIONS.—cont-continue; dec-decrease; inc-increase; k-knit; M-Main colour; p-purl; rem-remaining; rep-repeat; st(s)-stitch(es); yrh-yarn round hook.

FRONT.—With 2¾ mm (12) needles and M cast on 114(126) sts and work in k1, p1 rib for 13 cm [5 inches]. On the last row change to 3¾ mm (9) needle and dec evenly across this row to 92(102) sts.

Slip all sts on to a 4 mm (8) Tunisian hook. Join in A at left hand side of work.

next row: yrh, draw loop through first st, * yrh and draw loop through 2 sts; rep from * to end, 1 turning ch.

NOTE Tunisian crochet is worked over an outward and return row and these two rows are counted as 1 row.

Foundation row: (outward) hook in 2nd vertical st, yrh, bring up 1 loop, hook from right to left through middle of next 4 vertical sts and leave these sts on hook without working them, * take up 1 loop through each of the next 2 vertical sts, hook through following 4 vertical sts and leave on hook without working; rep from * to end taking up 1 loop through each of the last 2 sts.

Foundation row: (return) yrh and slip off 1 loop for the edge, yrh and slip off 2 loops, * yrh and slip off 5 loops (the working st and the 4 unworked sts of previous row), yrh, slip off 2 loops, yrh, slip off 2 loops; rep from * to end and slip off last 2 loops for edge.

row 1: (outward) yrh, hook into 2nd vertical st, yrh, bring up 1 loop, * yrh (make 1), hook in space preceding group, (pull up 1oop) 3 times [6 sts on hook], yrh, hook in space following group, [pull up 1 loop] 3 times, 1 loop through each next 2 sts; rep from * to end of row.

row 1: (return) yrh, slip off 1 loop for edge, yrh, slip off 2 loops, * yrh, slip off 13 loops (the working st and two groups of 6 sts) made at sides of 4 st group) yrh, slip off 2 loops, yrh, slip off 2 loops; rep from * to end of row, 1 turning ch.

One outward and return row forms pattern.

INCREASE ROWS.—row 1: as return pat-

This figure-hugging jumper features eye-catching chevron stitch in three closely harmonized shades

tern row but making 2 extra ch at each end.

row 2: as outward pattern row but picking up the 2 extra sts at each end of previous row.

row 3: as return pattern row slipping extra 2 sts off singly.

row 4: as return pattern row but make an extra half pattern on 2 extra sts at each end.

row 5: as return pattern row.

row 6: as outward pattern row incorporating half pattern.

row 7: as return pattern row making 2 extra ch at each end.

row 8: as outward pattern row picking up extra 2 sts at each end.

row 9: as return pattern row but slip extra 2 sts off singly.

row 10: as outward pattern row but make another half pattern.

There should be 17(19) patterns. Work until there are 13 patterns in height.

Join in M and work these 10 inc rows 19(21) patterns.

Work 7 pattern rows.

Fasten off.

SHAPE ARMHOLES.—Miss 2 patterns, join in M and work to last 2 patterns, turn.

Work straight until 13 pattern rows have been worked.

Fasten off.

Join in B. Work 7 pattern rows.

DIVIDE FOR NECK.—Work as for outward pattern row, work 2 loops, a stitch group, 5(6) times, 2 loops.

Dec a half pattern at neck on each of 2 foll outward rows (2 loops, 4(5) patterns, 2 loops).

Work on these st until 18 pattern rows have been worked.

Finish off.

Miss centre 5 patterns and work other side to match.

BACK.—With 2¾ mm (12) needles cast on 108(114) and work as for Front dec evenly along row to 86(92) sts.

Work as for Front omitting neck shaping.

SLEEVES.—With 2¾ mm (12) needles and M, cast on 58 sts and work in k1, p1 rib for 30.5 cm [12 inches] inc 1 st each side of every 4th row until there are 86(92) sts and working last row on 3¾ mm (9) needles. Change to A.

Transfer stitches to 4 mm (8) Tunisian hook and work as for Back until 13 patterns have been worked. Change to next colour and work 7 patterns.

Fasten off.

Miss 2 patterns, rejoin yarn and work 1 row. Dec one half pattern on every alternate outward pattern row until 2(3) patterns remain.

Break off wool.

NECK RIB.—Sew shoulder seams. With set of 4 2¾ mm (12) needles pick up and k 130 sts.

Work in k1, p1 rib for 9 cm [3½ inches].

Cast off very loosely.

Sew cast off edge to inside of neck. Sew side and sleeve seams.

TWO COLOUR SWEATER

1 9 5 5

* V-necked sweater with a check effect worked in two shades of wool and a combination of double crochet and long treble. Knitted ribs are used for the cuffs, welts and V-neck edge

MATERIALS.—Emu Superwash DK: 11(12:13) 50 g balls Main colour; 10(11:12) 50 g balls Contrast colour; 5.50 mm (5) crochet hook; pair of $3\frac{1}{4}$ mm (10) knitting needles.

TENSION.—15 sts and 22 rows to 10 cm [4 inches] over pattern. NOTE: work sample on a multiple of 4 + 1 turning ch as given for Back.

STITCHES.—1. two colour 'check' pattern in trebles.

NOTE: when working in colour pattern carry yarn not in use loosely up side of work.

SIZES.—To fit chest 97[102:107) cm [38(40:42) inches]. Actual measurement 114(120:126) cm [45(47$\frac{1}{4}$:49$\frac{1}{2}$) inches]; length from shoulder 67(69:71) cm [26$\frac{1}{2}$:27:28)

inches]; sleeve seam 48 cm [19 inches]. Figures in brackets () refer to larger sizes.

ABBREVIATIONS.—alt-alternate; beg-beginning; C-contrast; ch-chain; cont-continue; dc-double crochet; dec-decrease; inc-increase; k-knit; M-main; p-purl; patt-pattern; rem-remaining; rep-repeat;sl.st-slip stitch; st(s)-stitch(es) tbl-through back of loops; tog-together; tr-treble; yrh-yarn round hook.

BACK.—With 5.50 mm (5) hook and M make 89(93:97) ch, yrh, hook in 2nd ch from hook and work 1 dc in this and all subsequent ch to end, 1 turning ch. This is the foundation row and wrong side of work.

row 1: 1 dc in each st to end.

row 2: as row 1.

Join in C.

row 3: With C, 1 ch, * 1 dc in first st, (1 tr inserting hook in next st 2 rows below) twice, 1 dc in next st; rep from * to end, 1 turning ch.

row 4: With C, 1 dc in each st to end.

row 5: (right side) With M, 1 ch, * 1 dc in first st, (1 tr inserting hook between 2 threads of contrast tr 2 rows below) twice, 1 dc in next st; rep from * to end, 1 turning ch.

row 6: With M, 1 dc in each st to end.

row 7 & 8: With C, repeat rows 5 & 6.

Rows 5-8 form pattern.

Cont in patt until back measures 34 cm [13$\frac{1}{4}$ inches] ending with a right side row. **

SHAPE ARMHOLE.—next row: sl.st over 6 sts, patt to last 6 sts, turn.

Cont in patt on rem 76(80:84) sts until armhole measures 23(25:27) cm [9(9$\frac{3}{4}$:10$\frac{1}{2}$) inches] ending with a wrong side row.

SHAPE NECK.—row 1: patt 30(31:32), turn.

row 2: sl.st over 3 sts, patt to end.

row 3: patt to last 3 sts, turn.

Work 1 row on rem 24(25:26) sts.

Fasten off.

With right side facing, miss centre 16(18:20) sts, join appropriate colour to next st and

patt to end. [30(31:32)] sts.
row 2: patt to last 3 sts, turn.
row 3: sl.st over 3 sts, patt to end.
Work 1 row on rem 24(25:26) sts.
Fasten off.

FRONT.—Work as given for Back to **.
ARMHOLE AND NECK SHAPING.—row
1: (wrong side) sl.st over 6 sts, patt 37(49:41)
sts, turn and cont on these sts for Right
Front.
*** Work 3 rows.
Dec 1 st at neck edge on next and every foll

4th row until 24(25:26) sts rem.
Work a few rows until Front matches Back to
shoulder. Fasten off.
With wrong side facing, miss centre 2 sts, join
appropriate colour to next st, patt to last 6
sts, turn.
Work as for Right Front from *** to end.

SLEEVES.—With M and 5.50 mm (5) hook
make 49(53:57) ch and work foundation row
as for Back. [48(52:56 sts].
Work in patt as for Back, shaping sides by inc
1 st at each end of every 6th row 10(8:8) times
then every foll 4th row 5(8:8) times, taking
inc sts into patt.
Work straight on these 78(84:90) sts until
sleeve measures 40 cm [15¾ inches]. Place a
marker at each end of last row.
Work a further 4 cm [1½ inches].
Fasten off.

WELTS.—With right side facing, 3¼ mm (10)
needles and M, pick up and k 109(113:117) sts
along foundation row of Back and work in
rib.
row 1: p1, * k1, p1; rep from * to end.
row 2: K1, *p1, k1; rep from * to end.
Rep these 2 rows for 8 cm [3¼ inches].
Cast off loosely in rib.
Do the same for Front.

CUFFS.—With right side facing, 3¼ mm (10)
needles and M, pick and k 55(57:59) sts along
foundation row of sleeve and work as given
for welts.

NECK BORDER.—Join right shoulder seam.
With right side facing, 3¼ mm (10) needles and
M, begin at left Front shoulder, pick up and
k70(72:76) sts down left side, 1 st at centre of
V (and mark this st), 70(72:76) sts up right
side then 50(52:54) sts across Back neck.
[191:197:207 sts].
row 1: k1, * p1, k1; rep from * to within 2 sts of
marked st, p2 tog, p1, p2 tog tbl, k1, * p1, k1;
rep from * to end.
row 2: *p1, k1; rep from * to within 2 sts of
marked st, p2 tog, k1, p2 tog tbl, *k1, p1; rep
from * to end.
Rep these 2 rows three times more then first
row again. Cast off loosely in rib, dec at V as
before.

TO MAKE UP.—Join left shoulder seam and
neck border. Insert sleeves, placing centre of
sleeve top to shoulder seam and joining seam
above markers to cast off sts at underarm on
Back and Front. Join side and sleeve seams.
See ball band for pressing instructions.

winter warmth

SWEATER WITH EDGED COLLAR

1957

** *This version of the traditional fisherman's sweater is made in a double crepe wool yarn and a simple half treble stitch. The collar, cuffs and welts are knitted in rib*

MATERIALS.—Sirdar Classical Double Crepe; 17(18:19:20:21) 50 g balls; 4 mm (8) crochet hook; pair of $3\frac{1}{4}$ mm (10) and 4 mm (8) knitting needles; 1 button.

TENSION.—22 sts and 12 rows to 10 cm [4 inches] over pattern using 4 mm (8) hook.

STITCHES.—1. half trebles worked in front and back loops alternately; 2. k1, p1 rib; 3, stocking stitch.

SIZES.—Chest 86(91:97:102:107) cm [34(36: 38:40:42) inches]. Actual measurements: 94 (99:104:109:114) cm [37(39:41:43:45) inches]; length 49.5(52:55:57:60) cm [$19\frac{1}{2}$($20\frac{1}{2}$:$21\frac{1}{2}$:$22\frac{1}{2}$: $23\frac{1}{2}$) inches]; sleeve seam 47(48:50:51:51) cm

[$18\frac{1}{2}$(19:$19\frac{1}{2}$:20:20) inches].

Figures in brackets () refer to larger sizes.

ABBREVIATIONS.—alt-alternate; beg-beginning; ch-chain; cont-continue; dec-decrease; foll-following; htr-half treble; inc-increase; k-knit; p-purl; psso-pass slip stitch over; rep-repeat; sl-slip; sl.st-slip stitch; st(s)-stitch(es); st.st-stocking stitch; tog-together

BACK.—With 4 mm (8) hook make a loose ch of 105(111:117:123:129). Miss 2 ch (counts as 1 htr), work 1 htr in next and each subsequent ch to end, 2 turning ch.

row 1: miss first st, * 1 htr in back loop only in next st, 1 htr in front loop in next st; rep from * ending with 1 htr in top of turning ch, 2 turning ch.

This row forms pattern.

Continue in patt until work measures 30.5(32:33.5:34:36) cm [12($12\frac{1}{2}$:$13\frac{1}{4}$:$13\frac{1}{2}$:14) inches] with right side facing.

SHAPE ARMHOLES.—Sl.st across first 7 sts, 2 ch, pattern to last 6 sts, turn. Now dec 1 st at each end of next and every foll alt row until there are 76(82:88:94:100) sts. Continue in pattern until work measures 49.5(52:55: 57:60) cm [$19\frac{1}{2}$($20\frac{1}{2}$:$21\frac{1}{2}$:$22\frac{1}{2}$:$23\frac{1}{2}$) inches] ending with right side facing.

SHAPE SHOULDERS.—Sl.st across first 10(12:13:15:16) sts, 2 ch,, pattern to last 9(11: 12:14:15) sts, turn, sl.st across first 11(12: 14:15:17) sts, pattern to last 10(11:13:14:15) sts, turn, sl.st across remaining sts.

Fasten off.

FRONT.—Work as for Back until 90(94:100:106:110) sts remain.

NECK OPENING.—Dec 1 st, pattern 40(42:45:48:50) sts and turn. Work on these sts for first side keeping dec at armhole edge correct on foll 5(4:4:4:3) alt rows then cont straight in pattern until work measures 43.5(46:49:51:54) cm [$17\frac{1}{4}$(18:$19\frac{1}{4}$:20:$21\frac{1}{4}$) inches] ending at front edge.

The ribbed collar and neck opening make this warm sweater practical as well as smart

SHAPE NECK.—Sl.st across first 8 sts, 2 ch, pattern to end. Now keeping pattern correct, dec 1 st at neck edge on every row until 19(22:25:28:31) sts remain, cont in pattern until work measures same as Back to shoulder, ending with right side facing.

SHAPE SHOULDERS.—Sl.st across first 10(12:13:15:16) sts, 2 ch, pattern to end, sl.st across remaining sts.

Fasten off.

Rejoin yarn to remaining sts, sl.st across centre 6 sts, work on remaining sts to match first side, reversing all shapings.

SLEEVES.—With 4 mm (8) hook make a ch of 53(53:65:65:65) and work in pattern as on Back **at the same time** and keeping pattern correct, inc 1 st at each end of foll third row until there are 78(78:94:94:94) sts, cont in pattern until work measures 37(38:39.5:41:41) cm [14½(15:15½:16:16) inches] ending with right side facing.

SHAPE TOP.—Sl st across first 10 sts, 2 ch, pattern to last 9 sts, turn, now sl. st across 4 sts at beg of next 6 rows, then sl. st across 3 sts at beg of every row until 22 sts rem, sl. st across remaining sts.

Fasten off.

WELTS.—(worked separately) With 3¼ mm (10) needles and right side facing, pick up and k 104(110:116:122:128) sts evenly along base chain, dec 14 sts evenly across first row. (90:96:102:108:114) sts. Work in k1, p1 rib for 5 cm [2 inches].

Cast off ribwise, allowing for natural ease.

CUFFS.—With 3¼ mm (10) needles and right side facing, pick up and k 52(52:64:64:64:) sts along base chain, dec 6(6:10:10:10) sts evenly across first row. Work in k1, p1 rib for 10 cm [4 inches].

Cast off ribwise, allowing for natural ease.

COLLAR.—Join shoulder seams. With 3¼ mm (10) needles and right side facing, pick up and k approx 84 sts evenly round neck edge. Work in k1, p1 rib for 15 cm [6 inches].

Cast off ribwise.

COLLAR EDGING.—With 4 mm (8) needles, cast on 234(230:238::246:238) sts and work in st.st as follows:

row 1: k 69(67:71:75:71) sts, k twice into next 2 sts, k 92, k twice into next 2 sts, k to end.

row 2: purl.

row 3: k 70(76:72:76:72) sts, k twice into next 2 sts, k 94, k twice into next 2 sts, k to end.

row 4: purl.

Cont in this way until there are 98 sts in the centre.

next row: knit, to form a ridge.

Now cont reading instructions in reverse, ie, sl 1, k1, psso, k2 tog, for each k twice into next 2 sts.

Work in this way in st.st until you are back to original sts.

Cast off loosely.

TO MAKE UP.—Set sleeves into place, easing any fullness. Sew into place. Sew side and sleeve seams. Pin cast on edge of edging to collar and centre front opening, right side together, with mitres at collar corners, sew into place, turn edging at ridge row and sl.st to seam line. Overlap ends of edging and sew to sl.st 6 sts at centre front. Fasten at neck with a button and button loop.

See ball band for pressing instructions.

CROCHET SWEATER

1982

* This easy-fitting sweater is shorter than the original knitted design. Here it is re-worked in a simple textured stitch with knitted rib for the collar, cuffs and welts

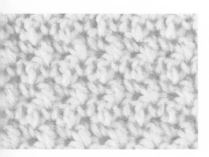

MATERIALS.—Robin Heritage DK: 5(6) 100 g balls; 5 mm (6) hook; pair of $3\frac{1}{4}$ mm (10) and $3\frac{3}{4}$ mm (9) knitting needles.
TENSION.—15 sts and 16 rows to 10 cm [4 inches] over pattern stitch 1.
STITCHES.—1. alternating double crochets and trebles; 2. k1, p1 rib; 3. garter stitch.
SIZES.—To fit bust 81-86(91-97) cm [32-34(36-38) inches]. Actual measurement 101(112) cm [40(44) inches]; length from shoulder 64(66) cm [25(26) inches]; sleeve seam 44 cm [$17\frac{1}{2}$ inches].

Figures in brackets () refer to larger sizes.
ABBREVIATIONS.—alt-alternate; beg-beginning; ch-chain; cont-continue; dc-double crochet; inc-increase; k-knit; p-purl; patt-pattern; rem-remaining; rep-repeat; sl.st-slip stitch; st(s)-stitch(es); tr-treble; yrh-yarn round hook.

BACK.—With 5 mm (6) hook make 78(88) ch, yrh, put hook into 2nd ch from hook and work 1 dc, * 1 tr in next ch, 1 dc in next ch; rep from * to end, 1 turning ch.
NOTE: pattern is reversible but for convenience, this foundation row is regarded as the wrong side of work. Begin pattern.
row 1: 1 dc in dc, * 1 dc in tr, 1 tr in dc; rep from * ending last rep 1 dc in tr, 1 dc in dc, 1 turning ch.
row 2: 1 dc in dc, * 1 tr in dc, 1 dc in tr; rep from * ending last rep with 1 dc in dc, 1 turning ch.
These two rows form pattern.
Cont in patt until back measures 32 cm [$12\frac{1}{2}$ inches] ending with a wrong side row. **
SHAPE ARMHOLE.—Sl.st over 2 sts, patt to last 2 sts, turn. Dec 1 st at each end of next 6(9) rows.
Work straight in patt on rem 61(65) sts until armhole measures 19(21) cm [$7\frac{1}{2}$:$8\frac{1}{4}$ inches] ending with a wrong side row.
SHAPE NECK.—Next row: patt 20(22), turn.
Next row: sl.st over 2(3) sts, patt to end. (18:19) sts rem.
Fasten off.
With right side facing, miss centre 21 sts, rejoin yarn to rem sts, patt to end.
Next row: patt 18(19) sts, turn.
Fasten off.

FRONT.—Work as for Back to **.
SHAPE ARMHOLES AND NECK.—Next row: sl.st over 2 sts, patt 33(38), turn.
Cont on these 33(38) sts for first side and dec 1 st at armhole on next 6(9) rows. **At the same**

The simple yet stylish sweater features both crochet and knitting

time, shape neck by dec 1 st at neck edge on 2nd row, then on foll 3 alt rows. Work 3 rows. Dec 1 st at neck edge on next row. Rep last 4 rows 4(5) times more. (18:19) sts rem.
Work 3 rows.
Fasten off.
With right side facing, miss centre 7 sts, rejoin yarn to rem sts, patt to last 2 sts, turn. Cont on rem 33(38) sts and finish as for first side.

SLEEVES.—With 5 mm (6) hook work 44(48) ch and work as for foundation row of Back. (43:47 sts).
Cont in patt as for Back and shape sides by inc 1 st at each end of every 4th row 12 times, then for **2nd size only,** inc 1 st at each end of foll 2 alt rows, taking inc sts into patt.
Work a few rows on these 67(75) sts until sleeve measures 38 cm [15 inches] ending with a wrong side row.
SHAPE TOP.—Sl.st over 2 sts, patt to last 2 sts, turn. Dec 1 st at each end of next 6(9)

rows. Work 1 row.
Fasten off. (51:53) sts rem.

COLLAR.—With $3\frac{1}{4}$ mm (10) needles, cast on 159(169) sts and work in rib.
row 1: (right side) k4, * p1, k1; rep from * to last 3 sts, k3.
row 2: K5, * p1, k1; rep from * to last 4 sts, k4.
Rep these 2 rows until collar measures 4 cm [$1\frac{1}{2}$ inches] ending with a first row.
Change to $3\frac{3}{4}$ mm (9) needles and cast off first 5 sts, cont in rib to last 5 sts, turn.
Cont in rib until collar measures 9 cm [$3\frac{1}{2}$ inches].
Work three k rows.
Cast off loosely.

WELTS.—With right side facing and $3\frac{1}{4}$ mm (10) needles, pick up and k 91(99) sts along foundation row of Back and work in rib.
row 1: (wrong side) p1, * k1, p1; rep from * to end.
row 2: k1, * p1, k1; rep from * to end.
Rep these 2 rows for 12 cm [$4\frac{3}{4}$ inches].
Cast off in rib.
Work the same for Front.

CUFFS.—With right side facing and $3\frac{1}{4}$ mm (10) needles, pick up and k 45(49) sts along foundation row of each sleeve and work in rib as for welts for 12 cm [$4\frac{3}{4}$ inches].
Cast off in rib.

TO MAKE UP.—Join shoulder seams. Join shaped edges of sleeves to shaped edges at armhole. Sew straight edge of sleeve to straight edge of armhole easing sleeve to fit. Sew cast-on edge of collar into neck opening. Join edges of garter stitch border together at centre front of collar, then sew first 4 cm [$1\frac{1}{2}$ inches] of collar neatly to base of opening at centre front. Join side and sleeve seams, reversing seam at cuff for 6 cm [$2\frac{1}{2}$ inches] for turn-back.
See ball band for pressing instructions.

CROCHET GLOVES

1 9 4 3

** *Warm gloves are worked in a soft cashmere and wool yarn with plain double crochet palms and fronts of the fingers, and popcorn stitch patterning the backs of the hands and fingers*

MATERIALS.—Jaeger Cashmere: 4 25 g balls; 2 mm (1) crochet hook.

TENSION.—7 sts and 8 rows to 2.5 cm [1 inches].

STITCHES.—1. popcorn stitch; 2. double crochet.

SIZE.—To fit average size hand.

ABBREVIATIONS.—beg-beginning; ch-chain; dc-double crochet; patt-pattern; rep-repeat; tr-treble.

RIGHT GLOVE.—Make Palm (beginning at outer edge of 4th finger). With 2 mm (1) hook, make 59 ch.

row 1: work 1 dc in second ch from hook and all subsequent ch to end, 1 turning ch. 58 dc. Mark other end with a coloured thread for wrist.

row 2: * 1 dc in back loop of next dc, 1 dc in front loop of next dc; rep from * to end, 1 turning ch.

row 3: * 1 dc in front loop of next dc, 1 dc in back loop of next dc; rep from * to end, 1 turning ch.

Rep last 2 rows until 6 rows in all have been worked ending at wrist.

BEGIN 3rd FINGER.—Work in patt across 42 dc, ch 21, turn.

next row: work 1 dc in 2nd ch from hook and all subsequent ch, work in patt to end, 1 turning ch.

Work 6 more rows ending at wrist.

BEGIN 2nd FINGER.—next row: work across 42 dc, ch 23, turn.

next row: work 1 dc in 2nd ch from hook and all subsequent ch, work in patt to end, 1 turning ch.

Work one more row ending at top of 2nd finger.

next row: work to within 14 sts of wrist, turn.

next row: work to end, 1 turning ch.

next row: work to within 22 sts of wrist, turn.

next row: work to end, 1 turning ch.

next row: work to within 30 sts of wrist, ch 21 for inner part of thumb, turn.

next row: work 1 dc in 2nd ch from hook and all subsequent ch, work to top of 2nd finger. Fasten off.

BEGIN 1st FINGER.—Ch 20, miss first 22 dc for 2nd finger, join and work in patt across part of palm and inner part of thumb, 1 turning ch.

Continue to work on these sts until 6 rows have been worked for 1st finger. Fasten off.

WORK OUTER SIDE OF THUMB.—Attach yarn to last st of ch at top of thumb and work over other side of this ch and remaining dc of palm to wrist. Work in patt

until 11 rows have been worked ending at wrist.

next row: work in patt to within 20 sts of end, miss these 20 sts and work in patt over remaining sts of palm and first finger.

Fasten off.

MAKE BACK.—Beg at outer edge of 1st finger, make 63 ch.

row 1: 1 dc in 2nd ch from hook, 1 dc in each next 9 sts, * [5 tr in next st, drop loop from hook, hook in top of first 5 tr and pull loop through forming a popcorn], 1 dc in each next 11 sts; rep from * three more times, 1 popcorn in next st, 1 dc in each next 3 sts, 1 turning ch. 62 sts.

row 2: 1 dc in each dc and popcorn to end, 1 turning ch.

row 3: 1 dc in each next 4 dc, 1 popcorn, * 1 dc in each next 11 sts, 1 popcorn in next dc; rep from * ending with 9 dc, 1 turning ch.

row 4: as row 2.

Rep rows 1-4 throughout for pattern.

Work on in patt until 7 rows have been worked ending at top of 1st finger.

Fasten off.

BEGIN 2nd FINGER.—Ch 22, miss first 20 dc for 1st finger, join and work in patt to end, 1 turning ch. Work on in patt until 8 rows have been worked for 2nd finger ending at wrist, 1 turning ch.

BEGIN 3rd FINGER.—Work across 42 sts, ch 21, turn.

next row: 1 dc in 2nd ch from hook and all subsequent ch, work in patt to end, 1 turning ch.

BEGIN 4th FINGER.—Work across 42 sts, 17ch, turn.

next row: 1 dc in 2nd ch from hook and all subsequent ch, work in patt to end, 1 turning ch.

Cont in patt until 7 rows have been worked for 4th finger ending at wrist. Turn and work 1 row of dc round outer edges of glove ending at outer end of 1st finger at wrist.

Fasten off.

TO MAKE UP.—Place back against palm and sew the 2 pieces together round outer edges leaving a 2.5 cm [1 inch] opening at wrist on outer edge of hand. Sew thumb seam.

LEFT GLOVE.—Work palm as for right glove.

MAKE BACK.—Beg at outer edge of 4th finger, make 59 ch.

row 1: 1 dc in 2nd ch from hook, 1 dc in each next 3 ch, 1 popcorn, work in patt as set for right glove until there are 58 sts, 1 turning ch. Work on in patt until 7 rows have been worked ending at top of 4th finger.

Fasten off.

BEGIN 3rd FINGER.—Ch 20, miss first 16 sts for 4th finger, join and work to end, 1 turning ch. Work on in patt until 7 rows have been worked ending at top of 3rd finger.

Fasten off.

BEGIN 2nd FINGER.—Ch 22, miss 20 sts for 3rd finger, join and work to end, 1 turning ch. Work in patt until 8 rows have been worked for 2nd finger ending at wrist, 1 turning ch.

BEGIN 1st FINGER.—Work in patt across 42 sts, ch 21, turn.

next row: 1 dc in 2nd ch from hook and all subsequent ch, 1 dc in each st to end, 1 turning ch. Work on in patt until 7 rows have been worked for 1st finger ending at wrist. Turn and work 1 row of dc round outer edge of glove ending at outer edge of 4th finger at wrist.

Fasten off.

Make up as for right glove.

SIMPLE SLIPOVER

1 9 6 9

* *This very simple, sleeveless, V-neck slipover in a double knit Shetland yarn is worked with alternating rows of double crochet and trebles and edged with crab stitch*

MATERIALS.—Wendy Shetland DK: 7(7:8:8) 50 g balls; 4 mm (8) crochet hook.
TENSION.—5 sts to 2.5 cm [1 inch] and 7 rows to 5 cm [2 inches].
STITCHES.—1. double crochet; 2. trebles; 3. crab stitch.
SIZES.—To fit chest 97(102:107:112) cm [38(40:42:44) inches]. Actual measurement 102(107:112:119) cm [40(42:44:46) inches]; length from shoulder 61(61:62:62) cm [24(24:24½:24½) inches].
Figures in brackets () refer to larger sizes.
ABBREVIATIONS.—alt-alternate; ch-chain; cont-continue; dc-double crochet; dec-decrease; foll-following; tog-together; sl.st-slip stitch; st(s)-stitch(es); tr-treble; yrh-yarn round hook.

BACK.—With 4 mm (8) hook make 102 (108:112:118) ch fairly loosely, yrh, hook into third ch from hook and work a dc in this and all subsequent ch to end, 2 turning ch. 100(106:110:116) sts.
row 1: miss first st, 1 tr in back loop only of every next st ending with 1 tr in both loops in turning ch, 1 turning ch.
row 2: miss first st, 1 dc in back loop only of every next st ending with 1 dc in both loops in turning ch, 2 turning ch.
These 2 rows form pattern.
Cont in patt and work straight until work measures 39.5(41:41:41) cm [15¼(16:16:16) inches].
SHAPE ARMHOLE.—Sl.st across 7(8:9:10) sts, work to last 7(8:9:10) sts, turn. Dec 2tog at beg of next 12 rows. 74:(78:80:84) sts.
Work straight until armhole measures 21.5 cm [8¼ inches].
SHAPE NECK AND SHOULDER.—Sl.st across 7 sts, dec 2tog, work to last 9 sts, dec 2tog, turn. Repeat this row twice more. 26(30:32:36) sts remain.

FRONT.—Work as for Back until work measures 33(34:34:34) cm [13(13½:13½:13½) inches] ending with a tr row.
DIVIDE FOR NECK.—Work across 50(53: 55:58) sts, turn and cont on these sts. Finish this side first.
row 1: dec 2tog at neck edge.
row 2: work in patt to end.
Rep these 2 rows 5(5:6:6) times more and when side edge measures 39.5(41:41:41) cm

[15½(16:16:16) inches].
SHAPE ARMHOLE.—Sl.st across 7(8:9:10) sts, work to end.
Dec 2tog at armhole edge 6 times while cont to dec 1 st at neck edge on alt rows.
Keeping armhole edge straight, cont to dec at neck edge until there are 24 sts. Work straight until armhole measures same as for Back ending at shoulder edge.
SHAPE SHOULDER.—Sl.st across 7 sts, dec 2tog, work to end, turn. Work to last 9 sts,

dec 2tog, turn. Dec 2 tog, work to end.
Fasten off.
Work second side to match first.

TO MAKE UP.—Sew shoulder and side seams. With 4 mm (8) hook work a crab stitch edging thus round neck and armhole edges.
row 1: work in dc to end. Do not turn.
row 2: work in dc to end.
Fasten off.
See ball band for pressing instructions.

CREW-NECK SWEATER

1981

* Colour co-ordinated tweed and plain double knit wool give this simple sweater added style. It is worked in double crochet with knitted ribs forming the neck, cuffs and welts

MATERIALS.—Emu Superwash DK: 9(10: 11:12) 50 g balls Main colour; 1(1:1:2) 50 g balls Contrast colour 4.50 mm (7) crochet hook; pair of 3¾ mm (9) knitting needles.
TENSION.—9 sts to 5 cm [2 inches] and 5 rows to 2.5 cm [1 inch] over stitch 1.
STITCHES.—1. double crochet; 2. k1, p1 rib.
SIZES.—To fit bust 81(86:91:97) cm [34(36: 38:40) inches]. Actual measurements: 98(103: 106:111) cm [38½(40½:41½:43½) inches]; length to shoulder 67.5(68:68:69) cm [26½(26¾:26¾: 27¼) inches]; sleeve seam 46 cm [18 inches].

Figures in brackets () refer to larger sizes.
ABBREVIATIONS.—C-Contrast colour; ch-chain; dc-double crochet; dec-decrease; foll-following; inc-increase; k-knit; M-Main colour; p-purl; sl.st-slip stitch; st(s)-stitch(es); tog-together.

BACK.—With 3¾ mm (9) needles and C cast on 87(91:95:99) sts and work in k1, p1 rib for 7.5 cm [3 inches] using a larger needle for last row of rib. Change to 4.50 mm (7) hook and M then work 1 dc in each rib st to end of row. Work straight until work measures 46 cm [18 inches].
SHAPE ARMHOLES.—Sl.st across 8 sts, work to last 8 sts, turn. ** Work straight until armholes measure 21.5(23:23:24) cm [8½(9:9:9½) inches].
SHAPE SHOULDERS.—Sl.st across 9(10: 11:12:13) sts, dec2 tog, work to end. Repeat this row.
Sl.st across 10(11:12:13:14) sts, dec2 tog, work to end. Repeat this row. 25 sts remain. Fasten off.

FRONT.—Work as for Back to **
Work straight until armhole measures 15 cm [6 inches].
SHAPE NECK.—Work 28(30:32:34) sts, turn.
next row: dec2 tog at neck edge, work to armhole edge.
next row: work to last 2 sts at neck edge, dec 2tog.
Continue dec in this way until there are 23(25:27:29) sts, then work straight until armhole measures same as for Back.
SHAPE SHOULDERS.—Work as for Back. Rejoin yarn to other side of work leaving 15 sts at centre and work the remaining 28(30:32:34) sts as for first side.
Fasten off.

SLEEVES.—With 3¾ mm (9) needles cast on 50(54:54:58) sts and work in k1, p1 rib for 7.5

cm [3 inches] using a larger size needle and inc 1 st either end of last row. Change to 4.50 mm (7) hook and work 1 dc st in each rib st to end of row. Cont in dc increasing 1 st either side of every foll 10th row until there are 58(64:64:68) sts. Work straight until sleeve measures 46 cm [18 inches].

SHAPE TOP.—Sl.st across 8 sts, work to end; sl.st across 8 sts work to end. Dec 2tog at each end of next 2 rows then at the beginning of next 16(18:18:20) rows. Dec 2tog at the beg of next 2(4:4:5) rows.
Fasten off.

NECKBAND.—Join right shoulder seam. With 3¾ mm (9) needles, pick up and k approximately 100 sts round neck. Work in k1, p1 rib for 2.5 cm [1 inch].
Cast off loosely ribwise.
See ball band for pressing instructions.

CABLE EFFECT JACKET

1981

** Originally a knitted design, this jacket has been re-worked in double knit wool using relief crossed crochet trebles for the cable pattern and crochet ribs for the edgings

MATERIALS.—Patons Waverley DK: 23 (25:27:29:31) 50 g balls; 4 mm (8) and 5 mm (6) crochet hook; 6 buttons.
TENSION.—3 tr and 1 cable pattern to 4 cm [1½ inches] over stitch 2.
STITCHES.—1. double crochet; 2. relief trebles.
SIZES.—To fit bust/chest 86(91:97:102:107) cm [34(36:38:40:42) inches]. Actual measurements 104(108:112:116:120) cm [41(42½:44:45½:47) inches]; length from shoulder 68(68:69:69:69) cm [26½(26½:27:27:27) inches]; sleeve seam 56 cm [22 inches].
Figures in brackets () refer to larger sizes.
ABBREVIATIONS.—ch-chain; cont-continue; dc-double crochet; dec-decrease; dtr-double treble; htr-half treble; inc-increase; patt-pattern; rb/tr-yarn round hook, hook from behind from right to left round stem of stitch and complete in usual way; rf/tr-yarn round hook, hook from front from right to left round stem of stitch and complete in usual way; sl.st-slip stitch; st(s)-stitch(es); tr-treble; yrh-yarn round hook.

BACK AND FRONTS.— (worked as one piece) WELT.—With 4 mm (8) hook, make 20 ch, yrh, hook in 2nd ch from hook and work 1 dc in this and all subsequent ch to end, turn.
Work in back loop of dc only, cont in dc until 192(199:206:213:220) rows have been worked. Turn work on side and work 1 dc in each row to end, 2 turning ch.
Change to 5 mm (6) hook. row 1: miss first st, 1 rf/tr in each next 2 sts, * miss next 2 sts, 1 rf/tr in each next 2 sts, 1 rf/dtr in each of missed 2 sts (crossed stitches form cable), 1 rf/tr in each next three sts; rep from * ending with one tr in turning ch, 2 turning ch.
row 2: miss first st, 1 rb/tr in every st to end, ending with 1 tr in turning ch, 2 turning ch.
Rows 1 & 2 form pattern.
Work straight until work measures 46 cm [18 inches] or desired length to armhole.
DIVIDE FOR FIRST ARMHOLE.—Patt across 38(40:42:44:46) sts, turn.
Dec 1 st at neck edge until 24(26:28:30:32) sts remain.
Work straight until armhole measures 22(22:23:23:23) cm [8½(8½:9:9:9) inches]. Dec 7(7:8:8:9) sts at armhole edge on next 3 rows. Fasten off.
DIVIDE FOR SECOND ARMHOLE.— Starting at front edge, patt across 38(40: 42:44:46) sts, turn.
Dec 1 st at neck edge until 24(26:28:30:32) sts remain.
Work straight until armhole measures 22(22:23:23:23) cm [8½(8½:9:9:9) inches]. Dec

7(7:8:8:9) sts at armhole edge on next 3 rows, work to end. Fasten off.

With right side facing, miss 18 sts, rejoin yarn, work Back in pattern over 80(83:86:89:92) sts. A second 18 sts remain unworked.

Work straight until armholes measure 22(22:23:23:23) cm [$8\frac{1}{2}$($8\frac{1}{2}$:9:9:9) inches]. Sl.st across 7(7:8:8:9) sts at beg of next row, work to last 7(7:8:8:9) sts, turn. Cont dec 7(7:8:8:9) sts either side twice more.

Fasten off.

SLEEVES.—Work cuff as for welt for 45(45:52:52:59) rows. Turn on side and work 1 dc in each row. 45(45:52:52:59) sts.

Change to 5 mm (6) hook and work in patt inc 1 st at each end of every wrong side row until there are 87(87:94:94:101) sts. Work straight until sleeve measures 56 cm [22 inches].

Fasten off.

COLLAR AND FRONT BANDS.—With 4 mm (8) hook, make 9 ch and work in patt as for welt but working last st on each row as a htr. Work straight for approx 85 rows for front bands.

NOTE: Work buttonholes on row 6 then every 14th row.

SHAPE COLLAR.—Inc 1 st as a htr st at neck edge every 3rd row until there are 20 sts. Approximately 36 rows.

Work straight until work fits to centre back neck. Approximately 72 rows. Continue to work second side of collar to match reversing all shapings.

Fasten off.

TO MAKE UP.—Sew shoulder seams. Sew sleeves into armholes. Sew side and sleeve seams. Sew bands to front edges. Sew on buttons.

See ball band for pressing instructions.

114

CAR COAT

1 9 5 9

** *First shown as a knitted jacket but now re-worked in crocheted shell pattern for the main parts and stocking stitch for the nicely shaped shawl collar, front bands and cuffs*

MATERIALS.—Patons Waverley DK: 16(17:18:19) 50 gm balls; 5 mm (6) crochet hook; pair of 4 mm (8) knitting needles; 6 buttons.

TENSION.—3 patterns to 5 cm [2 inches]; 15 rows to 10 cm [4 inches] over stitch 2.

STITCHES.—1. stocking stitch; 2. shell pattern.

SIZES.—To fit bust 81(86:91:97) cm [32(34:36:38) inches]. Actual measurements: 97(102:107:112) cm [38(40:42:44) inches] length 68.5 cm [27 inches]; sleeve seam 46 cm [18 inches].

Figures in brackets () refer to larger sizes.

ABBREVIATIONS.—ch-chain; dc-double crochet; htr-half treble; k-knit; p-purl; rem-remaining; rep-repeat; sl.st-slip stitch; st(s)-stitch(es); st.st-stocking stitch; tr-treble; yrh-yarn round hook.

BACK.—With 5 mm (6) hook, make 90(93:96:99) ch, yrh, put hook in 3rd ch from hook and work (1 dc, 1 htr, 1 tr), * miss 2 ch, (1 dc, 1htr, 1 tr) in next ch; rep from * ending with 1 dc in last ch, 1 turning ch. 29(30:31:32) shell patterns. This forms the foundation row.

row 1: (1 htr, 1 tr) in first dc, * (1 dc, 1 htr, 1 tr) in next dc; rep from * ending with 1 dc in turning ch, 1 turning ch.

Row 1 forms pattern.

Continue in pattern until work measures 46 cm [18 inches] or required length to armholes.

SHAPE ARMHOLES.—Sl.st across 4 patterns, work to last 4 patterns, turn.

Work straight until armhole measures 23 cm [9 inches].

SHAPE SHOULDERS.—Sl.st across 3 patterns, work to last 3 patterns, turn, sl.st across 3 patterns, work to last 3 patterns. 9(10:11:12) patterns.

Fasten off.

BACK COLLAR AND FACING.—With 4 mm (8) needles, pick up and knit 26(28:30:32) sts from 9(10:11:12) rem patterns.

row 1: k twice into first st, k to last 2 sts, k twice into next st, k1.

row 2: purl.

Repeat these two rows 17(18:19:20) times more. 62(66:70:74) sts.

Work 2 rows.

row 1: k1, k2 tog, k to last 3 sts, sl.1, k1, psso, k1.

row 2: purl.

Repeat these 2 rows until 26(28:30:32) sts remain.

Cast off.

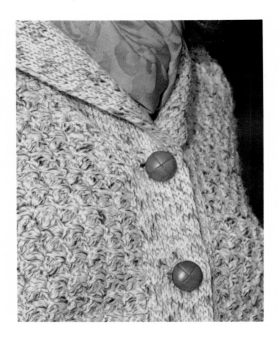

Simple stocking stitch bands and collar contrast with the pretty shell pattern crochet of the main body

LEFT FRONT.—With 5 mm hook, make 45(48:51:54) ch. Work foundation row. 14(15:16:17) patterns.

Continue in pattern until work measures same as Back to armholes ending at side edge.

SHAPE ARMHOLE.—Sl.st across 4 patterns, work to end. Put a coloured marker at this edge.

SHAPE NECK.—Ch 3 for turning ch, miss first pattern, continue in pattern to end of row.

Work 3 rows straight.

Continue to dec 1 pattern at neck edge every 4th row until 6 patterns remain. Work straight until armholes measure same as back ending at armhole edge.

SHAPE SHOULDER.—Sl. st across 3 patterns, work to end.

next row: work to last 3 patterns.

Fasten off.

RIGHT FRONT.—Work as for Left Front.

SLEEVES.—With 5 mm (6) hook make 51(54:57:57) ch. Work foundation row. 16(17:18:18) patterns.

Continue in pattern for 4 rows.

Inc 1 pattern either side of next and every 8th row until there are 24(26:28:28) patterns.

Work straight until sleeve measures 41 cm [16 inches].

SHAPE ARMHOLE.—Sl.st across 4 patterns, work to last 4 patterns, turn. 16(18:20:20) patterns.

Work 2 rows.

next row: ch 3 for turning ch, miss first pattern, work to end. Continue to dec 1 pattern at beg of each row until there are 3 patterns.

Fasten off.

FRONT BANDS AND COLLAR.—With 4 mm (8) needles, cast on 25 sts. Work in st.st.

row 1: k12, sl.1 purlwise, k12.

row 2: purl.

Repeat these 2 rows until band measures 2.5 cm [1 inch] less than left front to marker ending with a p row.

SHAPE COLLAR.—row 1: k1, k twice into next st, k to sl.st, sl.1, k to last 3 sts, k twice into next st, k2.

row 2: purl.

Repeat these 2 rows 10(11:12:13) times more. Now inc 1 st each end of every 4th row in same way until there are 73(75:77:79) sts. Work without shaping until edge measures same as front neck to shoulder.

Cast off.

Mark positions for 6 buttons on this band. Work another band in same way, working buttonholes to match markers as follows: k4, cast off 4, k4 including st. already on needle, sl.1, k4, cast off 4, k4. In next row, cast on 4 sts above cast off sts.

CUFFS.—With 4 mm (8) needles, pick up and k 52(56:60:60) sts along base of sleeve. Work in st.st for 5 cm [2 inches] ending with a k row. K next row to mark hem. Continue in st.st for a further 5 cm [2 inches].

Cast off.

TO MAKE UP.—Pin bands to Fronts, right sides together and oversew finely. Sew shoulder and collar seams. Fold front bands and collar to wrong side and sew over seam line with flat seam. Set in sleeves. Sew side and sleeve seams. Turn cuffs to wrong side at turning lines and sl.st.

Buttonhole round double thickness of buttonholes.

See ball band for pressing instructions.

crochet chic

BASKET PATTERN SUIT

1967

** *Crochet re-creates the classic 'Chanel' suit in a basket weave pattern using relief trebles. The slender skirt and long sleeved jacket are edged in contrasting double crochet*

MATERIALS.—Jaeger Matchmaker 4 ply: 22(24:26:28:30) 50 g balls Main colour; 2 50 g balls Contrast colour; 3 mm (10) hook; 20 cm [8 inch] zip fastener; 2.5 cm [1 inch] wide elastic for waist band; 4 buttons.

TENSION.—One 6 tr pattern to 2.5 cm [1 inch].

STITCHES.—1. Basket weave pattern; 2. double crochet.

SIZES.—Jacket: to fit bust 86(91:96: 102:106) cm [34(36:38:40:42) inches]. Actual measurements: bust 91(96:102:106:111) cm [36(38:40:42:44) inches]; length from shoulder 51(53.5:56:58.5:61) cm; [20(21:22: 23:24) inches]; sleeve seam 34(34:35.5: 35.5:35.5:37) cm [13½(13½:14:14:14½) inches]. Skirt: to fit hip 91(96:102:106:111) cm [36(38: 40:42:44) inches]. Actual measurements: 96(102:106:111:117) cm [38(40:42:44:46) inches]; length 69 cm [27 inches].

Figures in brackets () refer to larger sizes.

ABBREVIATIONS.—C-contrast; ch-chain; cont-continue; dc-double crochet; dec-decrease; inc-increase; M-main; patt-pattern; rem-remaining; rb/tr-yarn round hook, hook from behind and from right to left round stem of stitch, complete in usual way; rep-repeat; rf/tr-yarn round hook, hook from in front from right to left round stem of stitch, complete in usual way; sl.st-slip stitch; tr-treble, yrh-yarn round hook.

JACKET BACK.—With 3 mm (10) hook and M, make 110(116:122:128:134), ch, yrh, hook into third ch from hook and work 1 tr in this and all subsequent ch to end of row, 2 turning ch. 108(114:120:126:132) sts.

NOTE: turning ch counts as first tr for every row.

row 1: * 1 rf/tr in first 3 sts, 1 rb/tr in each next 3 sts; rep from * to end, 2 turning ch.

row 2: miss first st, 1 rf/tr in each next 2 sts, * 1 rb/tr in each next 3 sts, 1 rf/tr in each next 3 sts; rep from * to end, 2 turning ch.

row 3: miss first st, 1 rb/tr in each next 2 sts, * 1 rf/tr in each next 3 sts, 1 rb/tr in each next 3 sts; rep from * to end, 2 turning ch.

row 4: as row 3.

These 4 rows form pattern. Cont in pattern until work measures 30.5 cm [12 inches] or desired length to armhole, ending with 3rd patt row and omitting turning ch at end of last row.

SHAPE ARMHOLES.—Sl.st over first 9 tr, pattern to last 9 tr, 2 turning ch, turn. 90(96:102:108:114) sts.

Next row: keeping patt correct, miss first 2 tr, work to last 2 tr, miss next tr, work last tr, 2

turning ch.

Rep this row twice more. 84(90:96:102:108) sts.

Cont in patt without shaping until armholes measure 16.5(18:19:20:21.5) cm [6½(7:7½:8:8½) inches].

SHAPE NECK AND SHOULDERS.—Patt 20(23:26:29:32) tr, 2 turning ch. Complete this side first.

row 1: miss first 2 tr, patt to end, 2 turning ch.

row 2: patt to last 2 tr, miss next tr, work last tr, 2 turning ch.

row 3: patt to end, 2 turning ch.

row 4: sl.st over first 9(10:12:14:15) tr, patt to end.

Fasten off.

With right side facing, miss next 44 tr, rejoin yarn to rem 20(23:26:29:32) tr and complete to match first side, reversing shapings.

JACKET FRONTS.—(note: pattern is reversible) With 3 mm (10) hook and M make 56(62:68:74:80), yrh, put hook into third ch from hook and work 1 tr in this and all subsequent ch to end of row, 2 turning ch. 54(60:66:72:78) sts.
Cont in patt as given for Back [noting that there will be 9(10:11:12:13) 6 tr patts] until work measures same as Back to armhole omitting turning ch at end of last row.
SHAPE ARMHOLE.—Sl.st over first 9 tr, patt to end.
row 1: patt to last 2 tr, miss next tr, patt last tr, 2 turning ch.
row 2: miss first 2 tr, patt to end, 2 turning ch.
row 3: as row 2.
Cont without shaping until armhole measures 11.5(13:14:15:16.5) cm [4½(5:5½:6:6½) inches] ending at front edge.
SHAPE NECK.—row 1: sl.st over first 3 tr, patt to end, 2 turning ch.
row 2: patt to last 3 tr, no turning ch.
Rep these two rows until 18(20:24:27:30) tr rem. Cont without shaping until work measures same as Back to shoulder, ending at side edge with no turning ch at end of last row.
SHAPE SHOULDER.—Sl.st over first 9(10:12:14:15) tr, patt to end.
Fasten off.

SLEEVES.—With 3 mm (10) hook and M make 31(31:37:37:43), yrh, put hook into 3rd ch from hook and work as for Back. Cont in patt noting that there will be 5(5:6:6:7) 6 tr patts, for 18 rows. Break off yarn and work another piece in same way. Do not break yarn.
next row: work in patt, make 6 ch, then work in patt across 2nd piece.
next row: patt to end keeping continuity of patt across 6 centre ch, 2 turning ch.
first Inc Row: 1tr in 1st tr (1 inc made), patt to last tr, 2 tr in last tr (1 inc made).
Work 3 rows in patt.
Repeat last 4 rows, working incs into patt when possible, until 14(14:15:15:16) complete 6 tr patts are worked.
Cont without shaping until sleeve measures 34(34:35.5:35.5:37) cm [13½(13½:14:14:14½) inches].
SHAPE TOP.-Sl.st over first 9 tr, patt to last 9 tr, 2 turning ch.
next row: miss 2 tr, patt to last 2 tr, miss next tr, patt last 2 tr, 2 turning ch.
Rep last row until 40(40:46:46:46) tr rem with

no turning ch at end of last row.
next row: sl.st over first 6 tr, patt to last 6 tr, turn.
Rep last row 3 times more.
Fasten off.

TO MAKE UP.—Press under a damp cloth with a warm iron. Join shoulder, side and sleeve seams. Set in sleeves.

JACKET EDGING.—With 3 mm (10) hook and M, beg at lower right front side edge and work 1 row dc to front edge, working (1dc, 1 ch, 1 dc) in corner, work in dc up to right front neck, working (1 dc, 1 ch, 1 dc) in neck corner and cont in this way right round jacket.
Fasten off.
Join in C. Work 5 more rows of dc in same way. Fasten off.

SLEEVE EDGING.—Work as given for Jacket edging beg at one side of opening and working (1 dc. 1 ch, 1 dc) in corners. Fold one side of edging underneath other edging and sew to opening formed by 6 ch.
Finish top of sleeve opening with 2 buttons.

SKIRT BACK.—With 3 mm (10) hook at M, make 122(128:134:140:146), yrh, put hook into third ch from hook and work first row as given for Back.
Cont in patt noting that there will be 20(21:22:23:24) complete 6 tr patts.
Work 4 rows in patt.
first dec row: miss first tr, patt to last 2 tr, miss next tr, patt last tr (2 decs made).
Work 8 rows.
Rep last 9 rows until 19(20:21:22:23) complete 6 tr patts rem. Cont without shaping until work measures 51 cm [20 inches] or 18 cm [7 inches] less than desired length to waist.
SHAPE SIDES.—row 1: miss first 2 tr, patt to last 2 tr, miss next tr, patt last tr, 2 turning ch.
row 2: patt to end.
Rep last 2 rows until 90(96:102:108:114) tr rem. Cont without shaping until work measures 69 cm [27 inches] or desired length.
Fasten off.

SKIRT FRONT.—Work as for Back.

TO MAKE UP SKIRT.—Press as for Jacket. Join side seams leaving 20 cm [8 inches] open at last side for zip fastener. Sew in zip fastener. Join elastic to waist using casing st.

EDGING.—Work round lower edge as given for Jacket but omitting corner shapings.

THREE-QUARTER COAT

1 9 6 2

** Acrylic crepe double knit yarn is used for this three-quarter coat worked in an openwork pattern with bobble decoration. The sleeves are worked as part of the back and fronts

MATERIALS.— Robin Columbine Crepe DK: 19 50g balls; 3 mm (11) and 4 mm (8) crochet hooks; 4 buttons; optional 2.20 metres [2½ yards] lining fabric.
TENSION.—10 dc and 11 rows to 5 cm [2 inches] over stitch 1 with 4 mm (8) hook; 6 dc and 6 rows to 2.5 cm [1 inch] with 3 mm (11) hook; 11 spaces and 10 rows to 10 cm [4 inches] over stitch 2 with 4 mm (8) hook.
STITCHES.—1. double crochet; 2. bobble pattern.
SIZE.—To fit bust 86-97 cm [34-38 inches]. Actual measurement 112 cm [44 inches]; length 99 cm [39 inches] at centre back with edging; sleeve seam 33 cm [13 inches] with edging.
Figures in brackets() refer to larger sizes.
ABBREVIATIONS.—ch-chain; dc-double crochet; dec-decrease; inc-increase; rep-repeat; tr- treble; yrh-yarn round hook.

BACK AND FRONTS.—With 4 mm (8) hook, work 120 ch loosely.
row 1: 1 dc in fourth ch from hook, 1 dc in this and all subsequent ch to end of row, 2 turning ch. 118 sts.
row 2: miss first st, 1 dc in each st to end of row, 1 dc in turning ch, 2 turning ch.
Repeat row 2 five times more ending with 4 turning ch on last row.
next row: miss first st, 1 tr in next st, * 1 ch, miss next dc, 1 tr in next dc; rep from * ending with 1 tr in turning ch, 4 turning ch.
(59 spaces including the 4 turning ch).
START BOBBLE PATTERN.—row 1: 1 tr in first space, 1 ch, 1 tr in next space, 1 ch, yrh twice, hook in next space, draw loop through, (yrh, draw through 2 loops) three times, * yrh twice, hook in same space, draw loop through, (yrh, draw through 2 loops) twice; rep from * three times more (5 loops on hook), yrh, draw through 5 loops, turn, hook in top of first long tr and draw yarn straight through loop on hook (1 bobble), * (1 ch, 1 tr in next space) five times, 1 ch, 1 bobble in next space; rep from * to last two spaces, (1 ch, 1 tr in next space) twice, 4 turning ch.
row 2: 1 tr in first space, * (1 ch, 1 tr in next space); rep from * to end, 4 turning ch.
(59 spaces).
row 3: 1 tr in first space, * (1 ch, 1 tr) in next space four times, 1 ch, 1 bobble in next space, 1 ch, 1 tr in next space; rep from * ending last rep (1 ch, 1 tr) in next space five times, 4 turning ch.
row 4: as row 2.
These four rows form pattern. Continue in bobble pattern until work measures 70 cm [27½ inches] from beginning of bobble pattern ending with row 4 of pattern and 28 ch.
SHAPE DOLMAN SLEEVES.—row 1: 1 tr in fifth ch from hook, * 1 ch, miss 1 ch, 1 tr in next ch; repeat from * ten times more (12

spaces including turning ch). (1 ch, 1 tr in next space) to end of row. Join a separate strand of yarn to third ch st of row below. Work 24 ch. Work across ch (1 ch, miss 1 ch, 1 tr in next ch) twelve times. 4 turning ch.

row 2: as row 1 of pattern ending with 28 ch.

row 3: as row 1 for sleeve (107 spaces).

row 4: as row 3 of pattern ending work with 15 ch.

row 5: 1 tr in fifth ch from hook (1 ch, miss 1 ch, 1 tr in next ch) five times, (1 ch, 1 tr in next space) to end of row. Join another strand of wool to third ch of row below and work 12 ch. Work 6 spaces across ch, 4 turning ch. (119 spaces).

row 6: as row 1.

Work 17 rows ending with second row of pattern.

SHAPE NECK, SLEEVE AND FRONT.—

row 1: pattern over 50 spaces, 4 ch, turn.

Work 2 rows on these sts.

row 4: (1 tr, 1 ch, 1 tr) in first space (called inc 1), work to end, 4 turning ch.

row 5: work to end, inc 1, 4 turning ch.

Repeat rows 4 and 5 twice more ending row 9 with 7 ch.

row 10: 1 tr into 5th ch from hook, 1 ch, miss next st, 1 tr in next ch, (1 ch, 1 tr in next space) to end.

repeat last 2 rows once more.

row 13: work to end, inc 1. (62 spaces).

Work 6 rows.

row 20: work to last 6 spaces, 4 turning ch.

row 21: work to end.

row 22: work to last 12 spaces, 4 turning ch.

row 23: work to end.

Repeat last 2 rows once more. **

Work in pattern on remaining 32 spaces until Front measures same as Back to hem, ending with 1st row of pattern.

Work 7 rows in st.1.

Fasten off.

SHAPE LEFT FRONT.—Join yarn to centre of 19th space at back of neck.

row 1: work in pattern to sleeve edge.

Work two rows.

row 4: work to end, inc 1, 4 turning ch.

row 5: inc 1, work to end, 4 turning ch.

Repeat last 2 rows twice more.

row 10: work to end, ending with 7 ch.

row 11: 1 tr in fifth ch from hook, 1 ch, miss next ch, 1 tr in next ch, (1 ch, 1 tr in next space), work to end, 4 turning ch.

row 12: work to end, inc 1, work 7 ch, turn.

row 13: as row 11.

row 14: work to end, inc 1, 4 turning ch.

Work five rows.

Break yarn, rejoin to centre of 7th space from sleeve edge.

row 20: work to end, 4 turning ch.

row 21: work to last 12 spaces, 4 turning ch.

Repeat last two rows once more.

Now follow instructions for right side from **.

SLEEVE EDGING.—With 3 mm (11) hook, join yarn to sleeve edge. Work in stitch 1.

row 1: * work 3 dc in next space, 2 dc in next space; repeat from * along edge, 1 turning ch.

row 2: 1 dc in each st, 1 turning ch.

Repeat second row 15 times more.

Fasten off.

FRONT AND NECK EDGING.—Join yarn to lower edge of right front at beg of stitch 2. Work as for sleeve edging up front, round neck working 3 dc in each corner and down other side to stitch 1, 1 turning ch.

row 2: 1 dc in each st, working 3 dc into each corner, 1 turning ch.

row 3: as row 2.

row 4: work to right side of neck, ending with 3 dc in corner.

WORK BUTTONHOLE.—* 6 ch, miss next 6 sts, 1 dc in each of next 24 dc; repeat from * three times more, work to end, 1 turning ch.

row 5: as row 2, working 6 dc in each buttonhole.

Work three rows still inc at corners.

row 9: work to within 2 sts of corner st, insert hook into next st, draw loop through (2 loops on hook), insert hook into next st, draw loop through (3 loops on hook), yrh, draw through 3 loops (1 dec worked), dec 1, work to within 2 sts of left corner, dec 2, work to end.

Repeat last row 4 times more.

row 14: work to right side of neck ending at corner with dec 2.

WORK FACING BUTTONHOLES.—* 6 ch, miss next 6 sts, 24 dc; repeat from * three times more. Work to end.

Work 3 rows, dec at corners as before.

Fasten off.

TO MAKE UP.—Sew side and sleeve seams of crochet with a flat edge-to-edge seam. Turn up and slip stitch hem. Fold sleeve and neck edgings to wrong side and slip stitch. Buttonhole stitch round double thickness of buttonholes.

OPTIONAL LINING.—Using work as pattern, cut lining to match, having lining 5 cm [2 inches] less in length at hem and sleeve edges. Sew side and sleeve seams of lining and set into coat, sewing lining to inner edge of hem and facings.

See ball band for pressing instructions.

CROCHET STOLE

1 9 5 2

* This soft, warm, generously sized stole in easy-care acrylic yarn is worked in a linked cluster pattern and finished stylishly with long fringing at both edges

MATERIALS.—Sirdar Country Style: 7 50g balls; 4.50 mm (7) crochet hook.
TENSION.—4 complete patterns to 5 cm [2 inches].
STITCH.—Puff stitch pattern.
SIZE.—46 × 178 cm [18 × 70 inches] excluding fringe.

ABBREVIATIONS.—ch-chain; rep-repeat; tog- together.

STOLE.—With 4.50 mm (7) hook make 79 ch loosely.
row 1: miss 2 ch, * yarn round hook, hook into next ch, draw a loop through, yarn round hook, hook into same ch, draw 2nd loop through, miss 1 ch; rep from * once more (9 loops on hook), yarn round hook, draw through 9 loops, 1 ch (forming an eye), ** (yarn round hook, hook into eye, draw loop through) twice, miss 1 ch, yarn round hook, hook into next ch, draw loop through, yarn round hook, hook into same ch, draw 2nd loop through (9 loops on hook), yarn round hook, draw through 9 loops, 1 ch for eye; rep from ** to end of ch, 2 turning ch.
row 2: yarn round hook, hook into eye of last pattern of previous row, draw loop through, (yarn round hook, hook into eye of next pattern, draw loop through) twice, (7 loops only on hook at beg of each row), yarn round hook, draw through 7 loops, 1 ch for eye, ** (yarn round hook, hook in eye just made, draw loop through) twice, yarn round hook, hook into eye of next pattern, draw loop through, yarn round hook, insert into same eye, draw loop through (9 loops on hook), yarn round hook, draw through 9 loops, 1 ch for eye; rep from ** to end, 2 turning ch.
Repeat 2nd row loosely for 178 cm [70 inches].
Fasten off.

FRINGE.—Cut a piece of cardboard 18 cm [7 inches] deep, wind yarn round it and cut at one edge to form 36 cm [14 inch] strands.
Draw 6 strands through first space above starting ch, fold strands in half, * draw 6 strands through next space, fold in half then knot tog with 6 strands from previous space about 1 cm [½ inch] from stole edge. Repeat from * across each end of stole.
See ball band for pressing instructions.

ANGORA SWEATER

1965

* *Crochet is used to make the groups of flower petals in contrast yarn which are sewn over the body and sleeves of this soft, loose-fitting sweater knitted in stocking stitch*

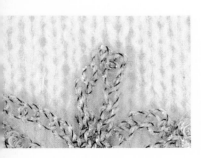

MATERIALS.—Avocet Angora and Elegance: 7(7:8) Angora 20 g balls; 2(2:2) Elegance 25 g balls; 4.50 mm (7) crochet hook; pair of 4.50 mm (7) needles.
TENSION.—22 sts and 26 rows to 10 cm [4 inches] over st. 1.
STITCHES.—1. stocking stitch; 2. chains and double crochet for petals.
SIZES.—To fit bust 81(86:91) cm [32(34:36) inches]. Actual measurement 86.5(94:101) cm [34(37:40) inches]; length from shoulder 60(60:60) cm [23½(23½:23½) inches]; sleeve seam 10 cm [4 inches].
ABBREVIATIONS.—alt-alternate; beg-beginning; ch-chain; cont-continue; dc-double crochet; dec-decrease; foll-following; inc-increase; k-knit; p-purl; rem-remaining; rep-repeat; sl.st-slip stitch; st(s)-stitch(es); st.st-stocking stitch.
Figures in brackets () refer to larger sizes.

BACK.—With 4.50 mm (7) needles and Angora yarn, cast on 86(94:102) sts and work 14 rows in st.st. Inc 1 st at each end of next and every 14th row until there are 94(102:110) sts. Work until Back measures 36 cm [14 inches] ending with a wrong side row.
SHAPE ARMHOLES.—Cast off 4 sts at beg of next 2 rows. Dec 1 st at each end of next and every foll alt row until 78 sts rem. Cont until work measures 24 cm [9½ inches] from beg of armhole shaping ending with a wrong side row.
SHAPE SHOULDERS AND NECK.—Cast off 4(4:4) sts at beg of next 2 rows.
next row: cast off 4(4:4) sts, k until there are 16 sts on needle, cast off next 30 sts, k to end.
next row: cast off 4(4:4) sts, p to neck edge.
next row: * cast off 4(4:4) sts at beg of next 3 rows.
Cast off rem 4(4:4) sts.
Join yarn to neck edge of rem sts and work from * to end.

FRONT.—Work as for Back until armhole measures 21 cm [8¼ inches] from beg of armhole shaping ending with a wrong side row.
SHAPE NECK.— K 24(24:24) sts, cast off next 30 sts, k to end.
Purl 1 row. * Dec 1 st at neck edge on next 5 rows, Work 1 row. Dec 1 st at neck edge on next row.
SHAPE SHOULDER.—Cast off 4(4:4) sts at beg of next row. Dec 1 st at neck edge on next row. Rep last 2 rows once more. Cast off 4(4:4)

sts at beg of next row. Work 1 row.
Cast off rem 4 sts.
Join yarn to neck edge of rem sts and work
from * to end.

SLEEVES.—With 4.50 mm (7) needles and
Angora yarn, cast on 60 sts and work 2 rows in
st.st. Inc 1 st at each end of next and every foll
alt row until there are 72 sts. Work straight
until sleeve measures 10 cm [4 inches].
SHAPE TOP.—Cast off 4 sts at beg of next 2
rows. Dec 1 st at each end of next and every
foll alt row until 38 sts rem. Dec 1 st at each
end of next 3 rows. Cast off 4 sts at beg of next
4 rows.

Cast off rem 16 sts.

TRIMMING.—With 4.50 mm (7) hook and
Elegance yarn, work 4 ch. Join to 1st st with a
sl.st to form ring. Work petals (12 ch, 1 dc in
ring) 5 times.
Fasten off.
Work 73 petal rings.

TO MAKE UP.—Sew shoulder seams. Set in
sleeves. Sew 30 petals to front, 31 to back and
6 on each sleeve. Sew side and sleeve seams.
With Elegance, work 2 rows of dc around
neck, sleeves and lower edge.
See ball band for pressing instructions.

DRESS AND JACKET

1965

** *Filet work is used for this easy fitting dress and matching jacket. The dress is sleeveless, the jacket has long sleeves, and careful stitch detail delicately outlines the neck edge on both*

MATERIALS.—Robin Columbine Crepe DK: dress 10(11:12:13) 50g balls; jacket 9(10:10:11) 50 g balls; 3 mm (10) crochet hook; 8 buttons.

TENSION.—12 tr and 6 filet spaces and 11 rows to 10 cm [4 inches].

STITCHES.—1. filet pattern; 2. double crochet.

SIZES.—To fit bust 86(91:97:101) cm [34(36: 38:40) inches]; to fit hip 91(97:101:107) cm [36(38:40:42) inches]. Actual measurement: bust 94(100:105.5:112) cm [37(39½:41½:44) inches]; hips 99(104:110.5:118) cm [39(41:43½:

46½) inches]; length of dress 95(96:96.5:97) cm [37½(37¾:38:38¼) inches]; length of jacket 51.5(52:53:53.5) cm [20¼(20½:20¾:21) inches]; sleeve seam 38 cm [15 inches].

Figures in brackets () refer to larger sizes.

ABBREVIATIONS.—Ch-chain; dc-double crochet; dec-decrease; inc-increase; patt-pattern; rep-repeat; sl.st-slip stitch; st(s)-stitch(es); tr-treble; yrh-yarn round hook.

DRESS BACK.—With 3 mm (10) hook make a loose ch of 141(145:153:159).

row 1: 1 tr in 3rd ch from hook and next 4(7:10:13) ch, * (1 ch, miss 1 ch, 1 tr in next st) six times, 1 tr in each next 11 sts; rep from * ending 1 tr in each last 6(9:12:15) ch, 3 turning ch. (Counting 3 turning ch as 1 tr, there is 1 group of 6(9:12:15) tr at each end with 5 groups of 12 tr and 6 groups of 6 filet spaces.)

row 2: miss first tr, 1 tr in each next 5(8:11:14) tr, * (1 ch, 1 tr in next tr) 6 times, 1 tr in each next 11 tr; rep from * ending with 6(9:12:15) tr, working last tr in turning ch, 3 turning ch. Row 2 forms pattern.

Work 7 more rows.

NOTE: if longer length is required, add extra length here.

row 10: miss first tr, 1 tr in each next 5(8:11:14) tr, * (1 ch, 1 tr) 6 times, work 4 more tr over tr panel, yrh, hook in next tr, draw a loop through, hook in next tr, draw loop through (4 loops on hook), yrh, draw through 3 loops, yrh, draw through remaining 2 loops [1 tr decreased, called dec 1 tr], 1 tr in each next 5 tr; rep from * ending with 6(9:12:15) tr over last group, 3 turning ch.

Work 9 rows having 1 st less in each of centre tr panels.

row 20: miss first tr, dec 1 tr, 1 tr in each next 3(6:9:12) tr, * work 6 spaces, 4 tr, dec 1 tr, 5 tr; rep from * ending 3(5:8:11) tr, dec 1 tr, 1 tr in turning ch, 3 turning ch.

Work 7 rows having 1 st less in each tr panel.

row 28: dec 1 tr in centre of each of the five 10

tr panels.

Work 7 rows.

row 36: miss first tr, dec 1 tr, work 5 tr, now dec 1 tr in each tr panel to end, 3 turning ch.

Work 5 rows.

row 42: miss first st, work 1 tr in each next 3(6:9:12) tr, now dec 1 tr in centre of next five 8 tr groups, work to end, 3 turning ch.

Work 5 rows.

row 48: miss first st, dec 1 tr, 1 tr in each next

1(4:7:10) tr, now dec 1 tr in centre of next 7 tr groups, dec 1 tr at end of last group, 3 turning ch.

Work 5 rows.

row 54: dec 1 tr in centre of five 6 tr groups.

Work 4 rows.

row 58: dec 1 tr at each end and 1 in centre of each 5 tr group, 3 turning ch.

Work 3 rows.

row 62: miss first tr, 1 tr in next 1(4:7:10) tr, *

(1 ch, 1 tr in next tr) twice, 1 ch, yrh, (hook in next tr, draw loop through) twice, yrh, draw through 3 loops, yrh, draw through 2 loops [1 space decrease], 1 ch, 1 tr in next tr, 1 ch, 1 tr in each next 4 tr; rep from * ending 2(5:8: 11) tr, 3 turning ch.

Work 6 rows.

NOTE: to inc, work twice into one st.

row 69: inc 1 tr at each end and 1 in centre of each 4 tr panel.

Work 3 rows.

row 73: inc 1 tr at each end of row. (2 incs).

Work 3 rows.

row 77: inc 1 tr in centre of five 5 tr panels.

Work 2 rows.

row 80: inc 1 tr in centre of five 6 tr panels. **

Work 4 rows or until desired length to underarm.

SHAPE ARMHOLES.—row 1: sl.st over 4(7:10:13) tr and 5 spaces, 1 ch, 1 tr in each of next 7 tr, work to end of last 7 tr panel, 1 turning ch.

Dec 1 tr at each end of 7 rows, 4 turning ch.

SHAPE NECK.—Work over 5 spaces and one 7 tr group, 2 turning ch. Dec 1 tr at neck edge every row 7 times. Work 3(4:5:6) rows on remaining 5 space group.

Fasten off.

Join yarn to first tr of second 7 tr group across centre, work to end. Now finish as for other side.

DRESS FRONT.—Work as for Back to **.
Work 1 row.

SHAPE BUST DARTS.—Break yarn and join to 4th tr of first complete 7 tr panel, 1 ch, 1 tr in each next 3 tr, work to last 7 tr panel, 1 tr in each of first 3 tr, 1 ch, sl.st in next tr. Break yarn, turn work and rejoin yarn to 6(9:12:15)th tr counting from side edge (1 ch, 1 tr in next tr) 3 times, 1 tr in each next 2 tr, 1 tr in 1 ch of join for first row of dart, 1 tr in each next 3 tr to within 7(10:13:16) tr of side edge, working 7 tr over bust shaping panel, 1 sl.st in next tr, break yarn, turn work. Join yarn to side edge, 3 ch, work in patt to end, 3 turning ch.

Work 2 rows.

SHAPE ARMHOLES.—row 1: sl.st over 4(7:10:13) tr and 5 spaces, 1 ch, 1 tr in each next 7 tr, work to end of last 7 tr panel, 1 turning ch.

Dec 1 tr at each end of next 4 rows.

SHAPE NECK.—row 1: dec 1 tr, work to end of first 5 space panel ending with 1 tr in first tr of 7 tr panel, 3 turning ch.

Now keeping neck edge straight dec 1 at armhole every row until 5 space panel remains (6 tr and five 1 ch spaces). Work until

armhole is same as that for Back.

Fasten off.

Join yarn to last tr of third 7 tr panel across centre and work other side in same way.

TO MAKE UP DRESS.—Sew side seams, work 1 row of dc round neck, armholes and lower edges. Press lightly; see ball band for pressing instructions.

JACKET BACK.—With 3 mm (10) hook, make 87(91:95:99) ch.

row 1: 1 tr in third ch from hook and all subsequent ch to end counting turning ch as 1 tr, 3 turning ch. (85:89:93:97 tr).

row 2: miss first st, 1 tr in each st to end with 1 tr in turning ch, 3 turning ch.

row 3: 1 tr in 3rd st, * 1 ch, miss 1 tr, 1 tr in next tr; rep from * ending last repeat with 1 tr in turning ch, 3 turning ch.

row 4: miss 1 ch space, * 1 tr in next tr, 1 ch, miss 1 space; rep from * ending with 1 tr in turning ch, 3 turning ch.

row 5: as row 4. **

row 6: *1 tr in 1 ch space, 1 tr in next tr; rep

from * ending with 1 tr in turning ch, 1 tr in 2nd turning ch, 3 turning ch.

Rep row 2 three times then 3rd, 4th, 5th and sixth rows once.

row 14: as row 2.

Rep row 2 for main part and work until Back measures 35.5 cm [14 inches] or desired length to armholes.

SHAPE ARMHOLES.—Sl.st over 4 tr, 2 ch, 1 tr in next and all subsequent sts to last 5 tr, 1 ch, sl.st in next tr, 2 turning ch.

Dec 1 tr at each end of every row until 61(65:69:73) sts remain. Work 4(5:6:7) more rows.

(Including 1st row of armhole shaping there will be 13(14:15:16) rows from armhole).

BEGIN NECK TRIM.—row 1: counting turning ch as 1 tr, work 9(11:13:15) tr, (1 ch, miss 1 tr, 1 tr in next tr) 22 times. Work remaining 8(10:12:14) tr, 2 turning ch. Keeping centre pattern correct work 2 more rows.

SHAPE SHOULDERS.—row 1: sl.st over 4(6:8:10) tr, 1 ch, 1 tr in each next 5 tr, work 3 filets, 3 turning ch.

row 2: 1 tr in 2nd tr, (1 ch, 1 tr in next tr) twice, 1 ch, sl.st in next tr.

Fasten off.

Count off 15 tr across centre, join yarn in 16th tr, and work 3 ch.

LEFT SHOULDER.—(1 tr in next tr, 1 ch) twice, 1 tr in each next 5 tr, 1 ch, sl.st in next tr, turn.

next row: sl.st over 1 ch and 4 tr, (1 ch, 1 tr in next tr) 3 times, 1 ch, 1 tr in turning ch. - Fasten off.

JACKET LEFT FRONT.—With 3 mm (3) hook make 41(45:49:53) ch and work as for Back to ** having 39(43:47:51) tr.

row 6: 1 tr in 2nd tr, (1 ch, 1 tr in next tr) twice, * 1 tr in 1 ch, 1 tr in next tr; rep from * ending 1 tr in 2nd turning ch, 3 turning ch. There should be 3 filet spaces at beg of row and 33(37:41:45) tr. Work 3 more rows.

row 10: work 3 filet spaces and 8 more tr (making a panel of 9 tr). Work 12(14:16:18) filet spaces to end, 3 turning ch.

Work 2 more rows in this way.

row 13: 1 tr in 1 ch, 1 tr in next tr over 9(11:13:15) filet spaces, (19(23:27:31) tr in all includng turning ch) work 3 spaces, 9 tr, 3 spaces, 3 turning ch.

Keep panels in this way and work until Front measures same as Back to armholes ending at front edge.

SHAPE ARMHOLE.—next row: work to last 4(6:8:10) tr, 2 ch, turn.

Dec 1 tr at armhole every row until 9(11:13:15) tr remain at armhole edge.

WORK NECK EDGING.—next row: work trs to first filet panel, work 10 filet spaces to end.

Work 2 more rows ending at front edge.

SHAPE NECK.—Break yarn, turn and rejoin to 8th tr from front edge, 3 ch, 1 tr in next tr, 1 ch, 1 tr, 1 ch, 1 tr in each of last 9(11:13:15) tr, 3 turning ch.

Work 7(8:7:8) more rows keeping 3 filet spaces at neck edge.

SHAPE SHOULDER.—Work as for left (right:left:right) side of Back.

Fasten off.

Join yarn to neck edge of front and work front edging.

row 1: * 1 dc in top of tr, 1 dc through bar of tr; rep from * down Front ending 1 dc in starting ch, 1 turning ch.

row 2: miss first dc, 1 dc in each st to end. (90 counting turning ch as 1).

Rep 2nd row 6 times more.

Fasten off.

JACKET RIGHT FRONT.—Work as for Left Front, reversing panels and shapings. For front edging beg and end at lower edge of Front, do not break yarn.

Sew shoulder and side seams. Beg again at lower edge of Front.

WORK BUTTONHOLES.—Work 1 dc, * 4 ch, miss 4 dc, 1 dc in each next 8 dc; rep from * six times more, 4 ch, miss 4 dc, 1 dc in last dc, 2 more dc in same space, work around neck edge, 3 dc in left corner, work down Front and lower edge working 3 dc in corners. Work 1 more complete round.

Fasten off.

JACKET SLEEVES.—With 3 mm (10) hook make 49(49:51:51) ch. Work as for Back to end of 6th row having 47(47:49:49) tr across first row. Cont in tr rows.

Inc 1 tr at each end of next and every following 4(4:4:3)th row until there are 59(63:67:71) tr. Work until sleeve measures 37 cm [14½ inches] or 1.5 cm [½ inch] less than desired length to underarm.

SHAPE TOP.—row 1: sl.st over 4(5:6:7) tr, work to last 4(5:6:7) tr, 2 turning ch.

Dec 1 tr at each end of every row until 35 sts rem.

next row: sl.st over 3 tr, work to last 3 tr.

Rep this row twice more.

Fasten off.

TO MAKE UP JACKET.—Sew sleeve seams. Work 2 rows of dc around lower edges. Set in sleeves. Sew on buttons.

See ball band for pressing instructions.

FILET PATTERN BLOUSE

1 9 4 9

*** *A fine cotton filet pattern is used for the main part of this neat blouse set on to a double crochet waistband. The sleeves are worked in one with the front and back*

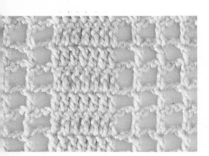

MATERIALS.—DMC Maeva crochet cotton: 3(3:4) 100g balls; 1.50 mm (2½) crochet hook; 16(18:19) small buttons.

TENSION.—11 sts and 5 rows to 2.5cm [1 inch] over pattern.

STITCHES.—1. double crochet; 2. filet pattern.

SIZES.—To fit bust 81(86:91) cm [32(34:36) inches]. Actual measurements: 81(86:91) cm [32(34:36) inches]; length 42(46:49.5) cm [16½(18:19½) inches].

Figures in brackets () refer to larger sizes.

ABBREVIATIONS.—ch-chain; dc-double crochet; dec-decrease; inc-increase; tr-treble; yrh-yarn round hook.

INSTRUCTIONS.—
FRONT WAISTBAND.—With 1.50 mm (2½) hook make 135(147:155) ch, yrh, hook in second ch from hook and work 1 dc in this and all subsequent ch to end of row, 1 turning ch. 133(145:153) sts. Work 6.5(7.5:7.5) cm [2½ (3:3) inches] in dc. Change to filet pattern.

For size 81 cm [32 inches] work first row as follows: 2 ch, miss first st, 1 tr in next st, 1 tr in each next 5 sts, * 2 ch, miss 1 st, 1 tr in next st (makes 1 mesh), make 3 more mesh, 1 tr in each of next 6 sts; rep from * to end, 2 turning ch.

NOTE: make 2 ch to turn at beg of row that starts with a tr; make 4 ch to turn for rows starting with a mesh.

For size 86 cm [34 inches] work first row as follows: 1 tr in 3rd st, 2 ch, miss 1 st, 1 tr in next st, 2 ch, miss 1 st, * 1 tr in each next 7 sts, (2 ch, miss 1 st, 1 tr in next st) three times, 2 ch, miss 1 st; rep from * to last 13 sts, 7 tr, (2 ch, miss 1 st, 1 tr in next st) three times, 4 ch, turn.

For size 91 cm [36 inches] work first row as follows: 1 tr in each of 2nd and 3rd sts, * (2 ch, miss 1 st, 1 tr in next st) three times, 2 ch, miss 1 st, 1 tr in next 7 sts; rep from * to last 10 sts, (2 ch, miss 1 st, 1 tr in next st) three times, 2 ch, miss 1 st, 3 tr, 2 ch, turn.

These first rows form pattern.

Work 10 rows in pattern.

Inc 1 each end of next and every 8th row until row begins and ends with 3 mesh(3 tr:2 mesh). Work without shaping until Front measures 20(21.5:25.5) cm [8(8½:10) inches] from waistband.

BEGIN SLEEVES.—Work 52(62:68) ch. Work 1 tr in 3rd ch from hook, 1 tr in each next 5 ch sts, continue in filet pattern to end of row.

Join a separate piece of yarn to last st of

previous row and work 50(60:66) ch for other sleeve. Now work across these sts with main yarn. 18(20:22) panels of 7 tr. Work on all sts until sleeve edges measure 12.5(13:14) cm [5(5¼:5½) inches].

SHAPE NECK.—Work across 7 tr and 7 mesh(8 tr and 8 mesh:9 tr and 8½ mesh) panels, 4 ch, turn. Finish this side first.

** Work 4(4:4.5)cm [1½(1½:1¾) inches] ending at neck edge. Join a separate piece of yarn to last st of preceding row and work 24(24:28) ch for back of neck. Now work across these sts with main yarn, ending with 2 mesh, 4 ch. Turn.

Work without shaping until sleeve measures 32(33.5:35) cm [12½(13¼:13¾) inches] ending at centre Back.

next row: work 2 mesh(6tr:4 mesh) 4(5:5) times, 6 tr, 3 mesh(3tr:6tr, 2 mesh) 4(2:4) ch, turn. Work without shaping until side edge measures same as Front to last inc.

Dec 1 st at side edge in next and every following 8th row until work begins at side edge with 6 tr(3 mesh:3 tr).

Work until Back measures same as Front to waistband. Work 6.5(7.5:7.5) cm [2½(3:3) inches] in dc.

Fasten off.

Join yarn to neck edge of other side at beg(beg:2nd mesh) of 4th complete mesh panel from opposite neck edge and follow instructions from **.

TO MAKE UP.—Sew side seams together. With right side of work facing, join yarn to lower edge of left Back. Work 1 row of dc up left Back and round neck and 171(193:204) dc down right Back, 1 ch, turn.

MAKE BUTTONHOLES.—On right back, work 1 dc in next 2 sts, * 3 ch, miss 2 sts, 1 dc in each of next 9 sts; rep from * 14(16:17) times more, 3 ch, miss 2 sts, 2 dc.

Fasten off.

Press. Sew on buttons.

TWINSET WITH CROCHET EDGING

1965

*** An elegant and simply styled twinset knitted in 4 ply in a twisted stitch pattern is given additional impact by an openwork crochet braid edging in a contrasting colour.*

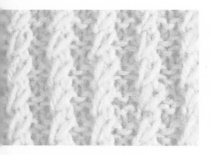

MATERIALS.—Wendy Ascot 4 ply: 17(18:19:20:21) 50g balls of Main colour; 1(1:1:1:1:1) 50g ball of Contrast colour; 3 mm (11) crochet hook; pair of 2¼ mm (13) knitting needles; pair of 3¼ mm (10) knitting needles; 10 cm [4 inch] zip fastener.

TENSION.—9 sts and 14 rows to 2.5 cm [1 inch] over stitch 1.

STITCHES.- 1. twisted rib; 2. openwork edging.

SIZES.—To fit bust 81(86:91:97:102) cm [32(34:36:38:40) inches]. Jumper length 47(47.5:48:49:49.5) cm [18½(18¾:19:19¼:19½) inches]; sleeve seam 10(10:10:11.5:11.5) cm [4(4:4:4½:4½) inches]. Cardigan length 53(53.5:54:54.5:55) cm [20¾(21:21¼:21½:21¾) inches]; sleeve seam 44.5(44.5:44.5:46:46) cm

[17½(17½:17½:18:18) inches].

Figures in brackets () refer to larger sizes.

ABBREVIATIONS.—alt-alternate; beg-beginning, C-contrast; ch-chain; cont-continue; dc-double crochet; dec-decrease; foll-following; inc-increase; k-knit; M-main; p-purl; patt-pattern; rep-repeat; sl.-slip; st(s)-stitch(es); st.st-stocking st; ybk-yarn back; yfwd-yarn forward.

JUMPER

BACK.—With 2¼ mm (13) needles and M cast on 146(154:162:170:178) sts. Beg with a k row work 7 rows in st.st.

row 8: k into back of all sts for hemline.

Change to 3¼ mm (10) needles.

row 1: k2, * k in 2nd st then k first st on left hand needle [called tw2], k2; rep from * to end.

row 2: k2, * p2, k2; rep from * to end.

row 3: k2, * sl.2 purlwise, k2; rep from * to end.

row 4: k2, * yfwd, sl.2 purlwise, ybk, k2; rep from * to end.

These four rows form pattern and are repeated throughout.

Work 10 cm [4 inches]. Cont in patt inc 1 st at each end of next and every foll 26th row until there are 154(162:170:178:186) sts. Cont without shaping until work measures 30.5 cm [12 inches] or desired length to armhole ending with a row 4.

SHAPE ARMHOLES.—Cast off 6(7:8:9:10) sts at beg of next 2 rows.

Dec 1 st at each end of next and every alt row until 126(130:134:138:142) sts remain. Work without shaping until armhole measures 9(9.5:10:10.5:11:11.5) cm [3½(3¾:4:4¼:4½) inches] ending with a wrong side row.

DIVIDE FOR BACK OPENING.—row 1: patt 63(65:67:69:71) sts, turn. Complete this side first. **

Work until armhole measures 16.5(17:18: 18.5:19.5) cm [6½(6¾:7:7¼:7½) inches] ending at armhole edge.

SHAPE SHOULDER.—Cast off at beg of next and every alt row 6(7:8:9:10) sts once, 5 sts seven times.

Cast off remaining sts. ** With right side facing rejoin yarn at inner edge of Back opening and work as for first side from ** to **.

FRONT.—Work as for Back until armholes measure 11.5(12:13:13.5:14) cm [4½(4¾:5:5¼:5½) inches] ending with a wrong side row.

SHAPE NECK.—row 1: patt 54(55:56:57:58), cast off 18(20:22:24:26), patt to end of row. Work this side first.

* Dec 1 st at neck edge on next 5 rows, then next and every alt row until 41(42:43:44:45) sts remain. Work without shaping until armhole measures same as Back to shoulder, ending at armhole edge.

SHAPE SHOULDER.—Cast off at beg of next and every alt row 6(7:8:9:10) sts once and 5 sts seven times. * With wrong side of work facing, rejoin yarn at neck edge and work as for other side from * to *.

SLEEVES.—With 2¼ mm (13) needles cast on 98(98:102:106:110) sts. Work 7 rows in st.st. row 8: k into back of all sts for hemline.

Change to 3¼ mm (10) needles and work in patt.

Inc at each end of 7th and every foll 8th row until there are 108(112:116:120:124) sts. Work until 10(10:10:11.5:11.5) cm [4(4:4:4½:4½) inches] ending with a wrong side row.

SHAPE TOP.—Cast off 6(7:8:9:10) at beg of next 2 rows. Dec 1 st at each end of next 6 rows then next and every alt row until there are 46 sts. Work 1 row. Cast off 3 sts at beg of next 10 rows.

Cast off.

TO MAKE UP JUMPER.—Join shoulder, side and sleeve seams. Set in sleeves. Turn hems to wrong side and sl.st.

CROCHET EDGING.—With 3 mm (11) hook and C, make 5 ch.

row 1: (1 dc in next st) twice, 2 ch, 1 dc in last ch, 1 turning ch.

Rep row 1 until strip is long enough for edge to be trimmed. Work 1 row of dc in M around neck. Sew edging round neck edge. Sew zip fastener to Back opening.

CARDIGAN

BACK.—With 3¼ mm (10) needles and M, cast on 158(166:174:182:190) sts. Work in patt as for jumper. Cont until work measures 35.5 cm [14 inches] or desired length to armhole ending with a 4th patt row.

SHAPE ARMHOLES.—Cast off 7(8:9:10:11) sts at beg of next 2 rows. Dec 1 st at each end of next and every alt row until 130(134:138:142:146) sts remain. Work until armhole measures 17.5(18:18.5:19:19.5) cm [6¾(7:7¼:7½:7¾) inches] ending with a wrong side row.

SHAPE SHOULDERS.—Cast off at beg of next and every row 6(7:8:9:10) sts twice, 6 sts twice and 5 sts twelve times.

Cast off remaining sts.

LEFT FRONT.—With 3¼ mm (10) needles and M, cast on 78(82:86:90:94) sts. Work in patt until work is the same length as Back to armhole, ending at side edge.

SHAPE ARMHOLE.—Cast off 7(8:9:10:11) sts at beg of next row.

Work 1 row.

Dec 1 st at armhole edge on next and every alt row until 64(66:68:70:72) sts remain. Cont until armhole measures 12(12.5:13.5:14:14.5) cm [4¾(5:5¼:5½:5¾) inches] ending at front edge.

SHAPE NECK.—Cast off 10(11:12:13:14) sts at beg of next row. Dec 1 st at neck edge on next 6 rows then on next and every alt row until 42(43:44:45:46)sts remain.

Work until armhole measures same as Back to shoulder ending at armhole edge.

SHAPE SHOULDER.—Cast off at beg of next and every alt row 6(7:8:9:10) sts once, 6 sts once and 5 sts six times.

RIGHT FRONT.—Work as for left Front reversing shapings.

SLEEVES.—With 3¼ mm (10) needles and M cast on 70(72:74:76:78) sts. Work in patt, inc 1 st at each end of 9th and every foll 10(10:8:8:8)th row until there are 114(118:122:126:130) sts. Work without shaping until sleeve measures 44.5(44.5:46:46:46) cm [17½(17½:18:18:18) inches] or required length ending with a wrong side row.

SHAPE TOP.—Cast off 7(8:9:10:11) sts at beg of next 2 rows. Dec 1 st at each end of next and every alt row until there are 44 sts. Work 1 row. Cast off 3 sts at beg of next 10 rows.

Cast off remaining sts.

TO MAKE UP CARDIGAN.—Join shoulder, side and sleeve seams. Set in sleeves. Work 1 row of dc round cardigan and sleeve edges. Make edging as given for jumper and sew round front edges.

See ball band for pressing instructions.

FRILLED GILET AND JABOT

1942

*** *Softly frilled gilet and jabot worked in a fine crochet cotton with trebles for the centre strips and a pattern of Solomon's knots for the frills. Tiny buttons add the finishing touch*

MATERIALS.—Coats Anchor Mercer-Crochet Cotton no.40: 40 g; 1.75 mm (2) Milward steel crochet hook; 70 cm [27½ inches] 3 mm [⅛ inch] wide Calypso double faced satin ribbon; 12 small, matching, pearlized buttons; Coats Drima thread.
TENSION.—First 4 rows to 2 cm [¾ inch].
STITCHES.—1. trebles; 2. Solomon's Knot.
SIZE.—Width of gilet approximately 25 cm [10 inches]; length of gilet at centre front approximately 46 cm [18 inches].
ABBREVIATIONS.—ch-chain; double cro-chet; patt-pattern; p-picot; rep-repeat; sl.st-slip stitch; st(s)-stitch(es); tr-treble.

GILET.—Beginning at lower edge, with 1.75 mm (2) hook, make 98 ch, hook in 4th ch from hook and work 1 tr in this and all subsequent ch to end, 3 turning ch.
row 1: miss 1st tr, 1 tr in each tr, 1 tr in turning ch, 3 turning ch.
Rep row 1 fifteen times more turning with 1 ch instead of 3 ch at end of last row.
row 17: 1 dc in first tr, * draw loop on hook up 1 cm [⅜ inch], yarn over hook and draw through loop on hook, insert hook between double loop and single loop of this ch and make a dc (a knot st made), make another knot in same manner (1 solomon's knot made), miss 4 tr, 1 dc in next tr; rep from * working last dc in top of turning ch (19 solomon's knots made), turn.
row 18: 1 solomon's knot drawing thread up 1.5 cm [⅝ inch], * 1 dc over double loop to right of next knot, 1 dc over double loop to left of same knot, 1 solomon's knot; rep from * omitting a solomon's knot at end of last rep, turn.
Rep row 18 until gilet measures 28 cm [11 inches] from row 18 to top.
NECK SHAPING.—First Side: row 1: work in patt over first 8 solomon's knots, turn.
row 2: 1 knot st drawing thread up 1.5 cm [⅝ inch], work in patt to end, turn.
row 3: 1 solomon's knot drawing thread up 1.5 cm [⅝ inch], work in patt to end, turn.
row 4: as row 2. (6 solomon's knots).
Continue straight until work measures 21.5 cm [8½ inches] from 1st row of neck shaping. Fasten off.
Second Side: row 1: miss 3 solomon's knots on last row of main section, attach yarn to next knot st, 1 dc over double loop to right of knot, 1 dc over double loop to left of knot, work in patt to end.
Work to correspond with first side having 1 knot st at beginning of rows at neck edge and

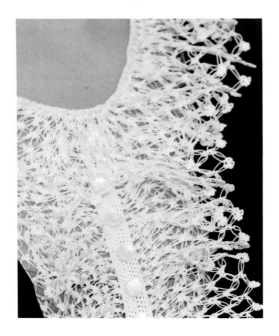

Twelve buttons add a formal touch to this frilly feminine jabot

keeping outer edge straight until there are 6 solomon's knots.

Complete to correspond with first side.

COLLAR.—row 1: with right side facing attach yarn to last row of one side of neck edge and work a row of dc neatly round neck edge keeping shape to fit neck and having an odd number of dc, 1 ch, turn.

row 2: 1 dc in each dc, 1 ch, turn.

row 3: 1 dc in each dc, 1 ch, turn.

row 4: 1 dc in first dc, * 1 solomon's knot, miss 1 dc, 1 dc in next dc; rep from * to end, turn.

rows 5-9: as 18th row of Gilet.

row 10: * 1 knot st, 3 ch, in dc of last knot st work (1 sl.st, 3 ch) twice and 1 sl.st (a triple p made), 1 knot st, 1 dc in centre of next solomon's knot; rep from * to end. Fasten off. With right side facing and keeping work flat work a row of dc neatly round remaining edges of gilet.

JABOT.—With 1.75 mm (2) hook make 91 ch.

row 1: 1 dc in 2nd ch from hook, 1 dc in each ch to within last ch, 3 dc in next ch, continue to work along other side of foundation ch, 1 dc in each ch to within last ch, 2 dc in next ch, 1 sl.st in first dc.

row 2: 2 dc in same place as sl.st, * 1 dc in each next 88 dc, 2 dc in each next 3 dc; rep from * omitting 2 dc at end of last rep, 1 sl.st in first dc.

row 3: 2 dc in same place as sl.st, 2 dc in next dc, * 1 dc in each next 88 dc, 2 dc in each next 6 dc; rep from * omitting 4 dc at end of last rep, 1 sl.st in first dc.

row 4: 1 dc in same place as sl.st, 1 dc in each dc, 1 sl.st in first dc.

row 5: 1 sl.st in each next 3 dc, 1 dc in next dc * 1 solomon's knot, miss 1 dc, 1 dc in next dc; rep from * to within last 7 dc, turn.

rows 6-10: as row 18 of Gilet.

row 11: as row 10 of Collar.

TO MAKE UP.—Damp and pin out the jabot to shape. Sew jabot neatly to centre front of gilet and sew buttons to centre of jabot spacing evenly. Cut ribbon in half and sew one length to each end of collar for ties.

COLLAR AND JABOT

*** Softly frilled collar and jabot worked in a fine crochet cotton. Double crochet is used for the centre strip and a loop pattern forms the delicate feminine frill*

MATERIALS.— Coats Anchor Mercer-Crochet Cotton no. 40: 20 g; 1.50 mm (2½) crochet hook; 1 button.

TENSION.—5 mm [1 inch] over first three rows.

STITCHES.—1. double crochet, 2. lace pattern.

SIZE.—Length of jabot 28 cm [11 inches].

ABBREVIATIONS.—ch-chain; dc-double crochet; rep-repeat; sl.st-slip stitch.

COLLAR.—To make the centre strip, make sufficient ch to fit round neck, 38 cm [15 inches] approximately, having a multiple of 3 ch plus 1.

row 1: 1 dc in second ch from hook, 1 dc in each ch to end, 1 turning ch.

row 2: 1 dc in each dc, 1 turning ch,

row 3: 1 dc in each dc.

Fasten off.

JABOT.—To make the centre strip, make sufficient ch to measure 23 cm [9 inches] approximately, having a multiple of 3 ch plus 2. With wrong side of collar strip facing, work 1 sl.st into centre dc on last row of collar strip, 1 sl.st into next dc, turn.

row 1: 1 dc in each ch to within last ch, 3 dc in next ch and continuing to work along other side of foundation ch, work 1 dc in each ch, 1 sl.st into each of next 2 dc on collar strip, turn.

row 2: 1 dc in each dc to within 3 dc group, 3 dc in next dc, 1 dc in next dc, 3 dc in next dc, 1 dc in each dc, 1 sl.st in each of next 2 dc on collar strip, turn.

row 3: 1 dc into each dc, 1 sl.st in next dc on collar strip.

Fasten off.

FRILL.—row 1: with right side facing attach yarn to first dc made on last row of collar strip, 5 ch, into same place as join work (1 dc, 5 ch, 1 tr), * miss 2 dc, into next dc work (1 tr, 5 ch, 1 dc, 5 ch, 1 tr); rep from * to last dc made on last row of collar strip, 5 turning ch.

rows 2-6: in first loop work (1 dc, 5 ch, 1 tr), * miss one loop, work (1 tr, 5 ch, 1 dc, 5 ch, 1 tr) in next loop; rep from * ending with 5 turning ch.

row 7: as row 6 omitting turning ch at end of row.

Fasten off

TO MAKE UP.—Damp and pin work out to shape. Sew button to one end of collar then make a loop at other end of collar to correspond with button.

SLEEVELESS DRESS

1968

* This ultra-simple, lightly shaped, sleeveless sheath dress with squared neck is worked in a lustre ribbon yarn and an easy alternating treble pattern. The length is easily adjusted

MATERIALS.—Avocet Soiree: 17(18:19) 50 g balls: 6 mm (4) crochet hook.
TENSION.—4 tr over 2.50 cm [1 inch] in width.
STITCHES.—1. trebles; 2. double crochet.
SIZES.—To fit bust 86(91:96) cm [34(36:38) inches]. Actual measurements: bust 89(94:99) cm [35(37:39) inches]; hips 94(99:104) cm [37(39:41) inches]; length 84 cm [33 inches]. Figures in brackets () refer to larger sizes.
ABBREVIATIONS.—alt-alternate; ch-chain; cont-continue; dc-double crochet; dec-decrease; sl.st- slip stitch; tr-treble; yrh-yarn round hook.

BACK.—With 6 mm (4) hook make 76(80:84) ch, yrh, put hook into third ch from hook and work 1 tr in this and all subsequent ch to end of row, 2 turning ch. 74(78:82) tr.
row 1: 1 tr in space between tr of previous row, 1 tr in turning ch, 2 turning ch.
This row forms pattern.
Cont straight in patt taking care to keep the same number of tr sts on each row until work measures 43 cm [17 inches] or desired skirt length. Then, every alt row dec 1 tr at each edge until there are 70(74:78) tr. Work straight for a further 23 cm [9 inches].
SHAPE ARMHOLE.—Sl.st across 5 tr, work to last 5 tr, 2 turning ch, turn.
Sl.st across 3 tr, work to last 3 tr, 2 turning ch, turn. 54(58:62) tr.
Work straight for 18 cm [7 inches].
SHAPE NECK AND SHOULDERS.—Sl.st over 14(15:16) tr, work centre 26(28:30) tr, sl.st to end. Fasten off.

FRONT.—Work as for Back until armholes have been shaped. 54(56:58) tr.
SHAPE NECK.—Work across 14(15:16) tr, 2 turning ch, turn.
Work straight on this side until it measures same as back to shoulder shaping.
Fasten off.
Miss centre 26(28:30) tr, attach yarn to 14(15:16) tr from opposite armhole and work to correspond to other side. Fasten off.

TO MAKE UP.—Sew side and shoulder seams. Work 1 row of dc around neck edge and around armholes.
See ball band for pressing instructions.

I RISH CROCHET VEST

1 9 6 8

*** *This design is made from separate motifs in an Irish crochet design and mercerised cotton yarn. The motifs are joined in as they are worked, to form a strip before making up the vest*

MATERIALS.—DMC Hermina cotton: 5(6) 50 g balls; 3 mm (10) crochet hook; 6 small buttons; lining material.
TENSION.—motif is 8 cm [3¼ inches].
STITCHES.—1. flower pattern motif; 2. double crochet.
SIZES.—To fit bust 81(86–89) cm [32(34–35) inches]. Actual measurements: 82.5(91) cm [32½(35¼) inches]; length from shoulder 56 cm [22 inches].
Figures in brackets () refer to larger sizes.

ABBREVIATIONS.—ch-chain; dc-double crochet; rep-repeat; sl.st-slip stitch; st(s)-stitch(es); tr-treble; yrh-yarn round hook.
NOTE: 1. squares are made and joined together in making this vest.
2. the vest can be lengthened — each additional 50 g ball makes 17 motifs.

FIRST STRIP.—FIRST MOTIF With 3 mm (10) hook, make 4 ch and join with a sl.st forming a ring.
round 1: work 8 dc in ring.
round 2: working through front loops only, work 1 dc in first dc, * 2 ch, 3 dc in same place, 2 ch, 1 dc in front loop of next dc (front petal made); rep from * until there are 8 petals, joining last 2 ch with a sl.st in first dc.
round 3: Working behind front petals in back loops of dc of round 1, 1 dc in first dc, * 2 ch, 2 dc in same place, 2 ch, 1 dc in back loop of next dc (back petal made); rep from * until there are 7 petals, work 2 dc in same place as last dc, 1 tr in next dc, turn, sl.st in last dc on round 1.
round 4: * (3 ch, 1 dc in top of next back petal) twice; 3 ch, 1 dc in same place (corner made); rep from * three more times.
round 5: * (4 ch, 1 dc in same space) three times, 4 ch, 1 dc in same place; rep from * three more times.
round 6: * (5 ch, 1 dc in next space) four times, 5 ch, 1 dc in same place; rep from * three more times.
round 7: * (6 ch, 1 dc in next space) five times, 6 ch, 1 dc in same place; rep from * three more times. Fasten off with a sl.st.
SECOND MOTIF.—Work rounds 1-6.
round 7: (ch 6, dc in next space) five times, 3 ch, from right side 1 dc in corner loop of first motif, 3 ch, 1 dc in same place on second motif, * 3 ch, 1 dc in next space of first motif, 3 ch, 1 dc in next space on second motif; rep from * until next corner loop is joined then complete the remaining 3 sides as for first motif.

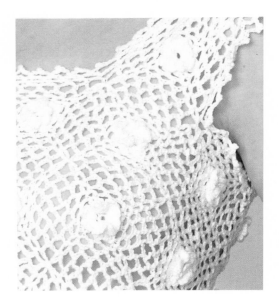

The motifs are worked separately, so the pattern can easily be lengthened if required

Continue to join motifs until there are 5 motifs in strip for length of vest to underarms by working a second motif then joining it on round 7, then completing the remaining 3 sides.

SECOND STRIP.—FIRST MOTIF Work as for second motif of first strip, joining to side of first motif of first strip.
SECOND MOTIF.—Work first 6 rounds as before,
round 7: (ch 6, dc in next space) five times, 3 ch, from right side 1 dc in next corner loop of first strip, join new motif to side of second motif of first strip; then join new motif to top of first motif of second strip, complete the motif as before. Continue to join motifs in this manner until 10(11) strips of 5 motifs have been joined.
Work 4 motifs for shoulder strap joining

motifs as given for First Strip and joining the strap to body of vest on 2nd and 4th motif from either side of centre back opening. Work another strap to match.

WORK EDGINGS.—CENTRE BACK OPENINGS.—With 3 mm (10) hook work 1 dc in first st, * (3 ch, 1 dc) in each loop to end.
row 2: work 1 dc in each st and each ch to end. Work 4 more rows of dc.
BUTTONHOLE ROWS.—on row 3, spacing buttonholes evenly, work 3 ch for each buttonhole.
on row 4: work 3 dc in each 3 ch space.
Fasten off.
NECK AND ARMHOLE.—With 3 mm (10) hook, work 1 dc in first st of side edging, then (3 ch, 1 dc) in each ch loop round neck ending with 1 dc in last st of second side edging.
next row: work 1 dc in first st then (5 ch, 1 dc) in each 3 ch loop ending with 1 dc in last st.
next row: 1 dc in first st, 2 ch, * work a 6 ch picot (6 ch, hook in 4th ch from hook and work a dc), 2 ch, 1 dc in each 5 ch loop ending with 3 ch, 1 dc in last st.
Fasten off.
Work armhole edges to match.
HEM EDGE.—row 1: 1 dc in first st, (4 ch, 1 dc) in each 6 ch loop to end, 1 dc in last st.
row 2: (5 ch, 1 dc) in each ch loop ending with 1 dc in last st.
row 3: 1 dc in first st, 2 ch, 1 dc in next ch loop, (6 ch picot, 2 ch, 1 dc) in each ch loop ending with 1 dc in last st.
Fasten off.

TO MAKE UP.—Sew in all ends. Block dress easing out to required width. Line vest allowing for ease.
See ball band for pressing instructions.

146

crochet techniques

GETTING STARTED

Standard crochet hooks are made from aluminium, plastic or bone, in various lengths from 15 cm [6 inches] to 20 cm [8 inches], and between 2 mm (14) and 10 mm (3). Some have handles and some people find these easier to use. Steel crochet hooks for finer work are available in sizes from 0.60 mm (6) to 2.50 mm (2). Tunisian crochet hooks are longer, usually about 30 cm [12 inches], with a knob at one end and a hook at the other, in sizes from 2 mm upwards.

Many of the yarns currently used for knitting are equally suited to crochet work, though bouclé and nubby yarns can cause problems, especially when several stitches have to be worked together. When you are choosing yarns, the size, the twist and the finish must be considered, and the yarn must be appropriate for the design to be worked. A tightly twisted yarn gives a firm finish, while a long-haired yarn will give a soft, fluffy finish. Fine yarns are best suited to delicate lacework, while thick, heavy yarns work best with bolder designs.

MAKING A CHAIN

Practically all crochet work begins with a chain foundation. To make a chain, first make a slip loop [fig. 1]. Hold the yarn in the left hand and make a loop with the right hand. Hold the loop in place between the thumb and forefinger of the right hand. Holding the crochet hook in the right hand, insert it through the loop and under the yarn.

Catch the long end of the yarn with the right hand. If you find it more comfortable, hold the crochet hook between thumb and middle finger, resting the forefinger near the tip of the hook.

Draw the loop through [fig. 2] and, leaving the hook in the yarn, pull the short end to close the loop round the hook.

Loop the yarn round the little finger, across the palm and behind the forefinger of the left hand. Pull the yarn gently so that it lies round the fingers firmly.

Catch the knot of the loop between the thumb and the forefinger. Pass the hook under the yarn and catch the yarn with the hook. This is called 'yarn over hook', the abbreviation for which is yoh.

Draw the yarn through the loop on the hook to make one chain. Continue in this way until the foundation chain is the desired length. The last loop on the hook is not counted as a stitch.

BASIC STITCHES

CHAIN

This is the foundation of crochet work. With the yarn in position and the loop on the hook as shown, pass the hook under the yarn held in the left hand and catch it with the hook. Draw the yarn through the loop on the hook. Repeat until the chain is the desired length. Do not count the original slip loop; count

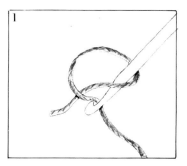
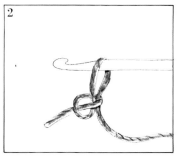
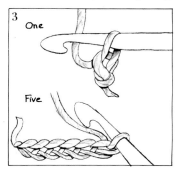

from the first chain made [fig. 3]. The abbreviation for chain is ch.

SLIP STITCH

Put the hook into the stitch to the left of the hook. Yarn over hook and draw through a loop. Draw this loop through the loop on the hook. When a number of chains have to be joined in a circle, the circle is closed with a slip stitch. The abbreviation for slip stitch is sl.st.

DOUBLE CROCHET

Begin with 1 chain for turning, then put the hook into the second stitch to the left of the hook. Yarn over hook [fig. 4] and draw through a loop. There are now 2 loops on the hook. Yarn over hook and draw through the 2 loops on the hook. Now 1 loop remains on the hook [fig. 5]. Continue working each stitch this way, omitting the turning chain. The abbreviation for double crochet is dc.

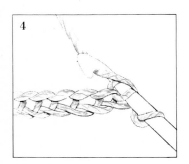

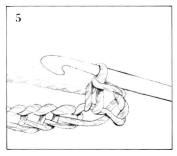

HALF TREBLE CROCHET

Begin with 2 chains for turning, then yarn over hook. Put the hook into the third stitch to the left of the hook, yarn over hook and draw through a loop. There are now 3 loops on

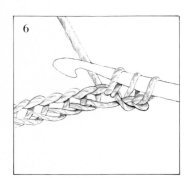

the hook [fig. 6]. Yarn over hook and draw the yarn through the 3 loops on the hook. Now 1 loop remains on the hook [fig. 7]. Continue working each stitch this way, omitting the 2 turning chains. The abbreviation for half treble crochet is htr.

TREBLE CROCHET

Begin with 3 chains for turning, then yarn over hook. Put the hook into the fourth stitch to the left of the hook, yarn over hook and draw through a loop. There are now 3 loops on the hook. Yarn over hook [fig. 8] and draw through 2 loops on the hook. Yarn over hook and draw through the remaining 2 loops. Now 1 loop remains on the hook [fig. 9]. Continue working each stitch this way, omitting the 3 turning chains. The abbreviation for treble crochet is tr.

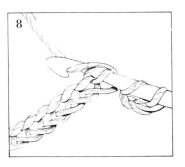

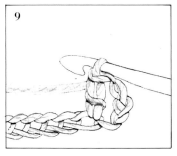

DOUBLE TREBLE

Begin with 4 chains for turning, then yarn

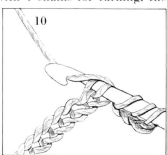

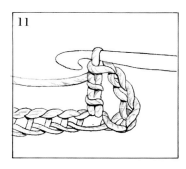

over hook twice. Put the hook into the fifth stitch to the left of the hook, yarn over hook and draw through a loop. There are now 4 loops on the hook. Yarn over hook [fig. 10] and draw through 2 loops on the hook. Yarn over hook and draw through the next 2 loops on the hook. Yarn over hook and draw through the remaining 2 loops on the hook. Now 1 loop remains on the hook [fig. 11]. Continue working each stitch this way, omitting the 4 turning chains. The abbreviation for double treble is dtr.

TRIPLE TREBLE

Begin with 5 chains for turning, then yarn over hook three times. Put the hook into the sixth stitch to the left of the hook and draw through a loop. There are now 5 loops on the hook. Yarn over hook [fig. 12] and draw through 2 loops. Repeat this three more times; that is four times in all. Now 1 loop remains on the hook [fig. 13]. Continue working each stitch this way, omitting the 5 turning chains. The abbreviation for triple treble is ttr.

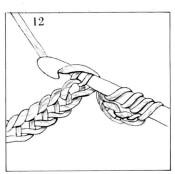

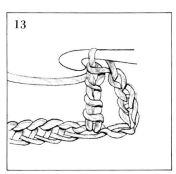

QUADRUPLE TREBLE

Begin with 6 chains for turning, then yarn over hook four times. Put the hook into the seventh stitch to the left of the hook, yarn over hook and draw through a loop. There are

now 6 loops on the hook. Yarn over hook [fig. 14] and draw through 2 loops. Repeat this four more times; that is five times in all. Now 1 loop remains on the hook [fig. 15]. Continue working each stitch in this way, omitting the 6 turning chains. The abbreviation for quadruple treble is qtr.

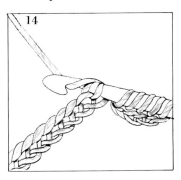

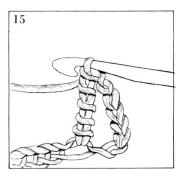

BASIC STITCHES FOR FILET CROCHET

Filet crochet designs are worked on a mesh usually made from a combination of treble crochet and chain stitches. The ground mesh is made by working 1 treble, 1 chain, miss 1 stitch, and repeating this to the end of the work. A wider ground mesh is made by working 1 treble, 2 chains, miss 2 stitches, and repeating this to the end of the work. The spaces are filled by working 1 treble in the 1 chain space and 2 trebles in the 2 chain spaces, a multiple of $2+1$ and $3+1$ respectively.

Start the ground mesh with 4 turning chains (this forms the first treble and 1 chain space) or 5 turning chains (this forms the first treble and 2 chain space).
The instructions for filet crochet are most often given in the form of a chart. The squares to be filled in are shown as *, x, or ● while the mesh ground is shown as an open square. It is important to remember that you are always

149

looking at the right side of the work when you are using a chart, so even number rows must be read from left to right.

There are two other constructions used in filet crochet: bars and lacets worked over 2 squares of the mesh. A bar is formed by working 5 chain stitches, missing 5 chains or a lacet, and then working 1 treble into the next stitch. A lacet is made by working 3 chain stitches, missing 2 stitches, 1 double crochet into the next stitch, 3 chain, miss 2 stitches, 1 treble into the next stitch.

BASIC METHOD FOR TUNISIAN CROCHET

Tunisian crochet differs from standard crochet in that, once the foundation chain has been worked, all the stitches are worked and kept on the hook to the end of the row. Then the stitches are worked back until there is just one stitch on the hook. Consequently, a special hook is required. This is longer than a standard crochet hook and has a knob on the end opposite the hook.

Many Tunisian crochet patterns start with the same two starting rows. These come from the first two rows of standard Tunisian stitch. Start with a foundation chain with the number of stitches required.

row 1 (outward): put the hook into the second

chain from the hook, yarn over hook, draw loop through and leave on hook, * hook into next chain, yarn over hook, draw loop through and leave on hook; repeat from * to end of row.

row 2 (return): without turning the work, yarn over hook, draw through a loop, * yarn over hook and draw through 2 loops on hook; repeat from * to end of work, 1 turning chain. [figs. 16–19]

row 3 (outward): miss first loop, * put the hook into the next loop, yarn over hook and draw through a loop; repeat from * to end of work.

row 4 (return): as row 2 (return).

DECORATIVE STITCHES

PICOTS

Picots are made from 3, 4 or 5 chain stitches according to the size of picot required. The final chain is joined to the work by working a double crochet into the first chain.

CLUSTERS

These are usually worked with treble or double treble stitches. Two or more stitches are worked in the same stitch, leaving the loop of each on the hook. Then the cluster is finished by taking the yarn over the hook and drawing it through all the loops. An extra chain can be worked to close them firmly. Clusters can also be worked over more than one stitch.

POPCORNS

Work one chain and then the number of stitches given in the pattern. Take the final

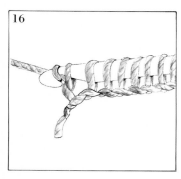

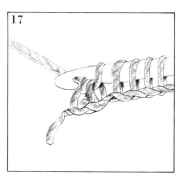

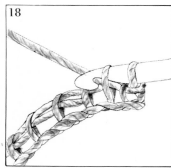

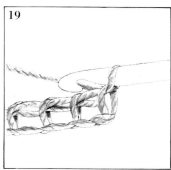

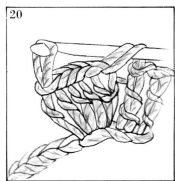

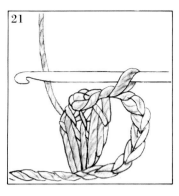

loop of the last stitch worked from the hook and put the hook into the one chain before the group of stitches, then into the dropped loop and draw the yarn through [figs. 20 and 21].

PUFFS

To work a puff, yarn over hook, put the hook into the stitch to be worked and draw yarn up 1 cm [3/8 inch]. (Yarn over hook, hook into the same stitch and draw yarn up) three times, yarn over hook and draw through all loops [figs. 22 and 23]. An extra chain stitch can be worked to close the puff more firmly.

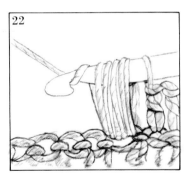
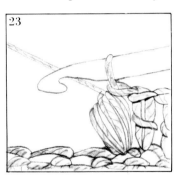

RELIEF STITCHES

These are worked by taking the hook round the stem of stitch. A relief front treble [fig. 24]

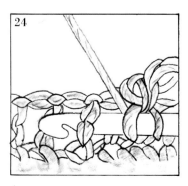

is made by wrapping the yarn over the hook, taking the hook from the front and from right to left round the stitch to be worked and then completing the stitch normally. The abbreviation for relief front treble is rf. tr.

A relief back treble is made by wrapping the yarn over the hook, taking the hook from the back and from right to left round the stitch to be worked and then completing the stitch normally. The abbreviation for relief back treble is rb. tr.

METHODS OF WORKING CROCHET

Crochet can be worked in rows or in rounds. When working in rows, it is necessary to work extra chain stitches to bring the hook and the yarn up to the level of the next row to be worked. The work is turned, as in knitting, to start the next row. When this forms the first stitch of the next row, it is important not to work into the first stitch of the new row.

The number of chains required to make the turning chain usually depends on the stitch being used. Sometimes it depends on the yarn. If the side edge looks 'pulled', try using 1 chain more. Otherwise, unless the pattern instructions give a different number, follow the list on page 152 for the number of turning chains required.

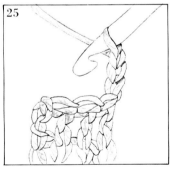

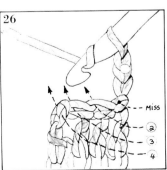

151

double crochet 1
half treble 2
treble 3
double treble 4
triple treble 5
quadruple treble 6

Crochet worked in rows is turned by means of these turning chains at the end of each row until the required length has been worked [figs. 25 and 26].

Crochet worked in rounds is joined by a slip stitch worked into the last stitch with the yarn pulled through the last stitch and loop on the hook, leaving one loop on the hook. The same method applies when working circular motifs. The initial chain is joined with a slip stitch and the next round is worked into this circle; each round is completed by means of a slip stitch into the first stitch of the round.

TENSION

As with knitting, tension is often the one element that is overlooked. However, it is essential to obtain the correct tension given in pattern instructions to get the desired measurements.

To check the tension, work a small square in the main pattern with the hook size specified. The sample should be at least 10 cm [4 inches] square; if the tension stated in the pattern is for 10 cm [4 inches], work a larger square. Put the sample on a flat surface and mark out the tension width of the pattern with pins. Count the number of stitches and rows carefully and

if the tension is correct, then you can begin work on the garment [fig. 27].

If there is the slightest doubt whether the tension is correct, work another sample square, using a smaller hook if there are fewer stitches than the required tension or a larger hook if there are more stitches than the required tension.

WORKING WITH MORE THAN ONE COLOUR

When changing from one colour yarn to another during a row of trebles, with the right side of the work facing and before drawing the yarn through the last two loops on the hook, take the new colour and put it over the hook, leaving the first colour at the back of the work. Then draw through the last two loops with the new colour. If the area of the second colour is small, the first colour can be left at the back of the work [figs. 28–31]. If the

27

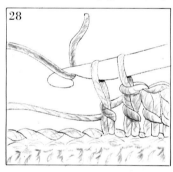

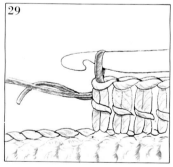

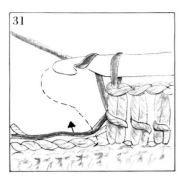

second colour area is made of several stitches, it is better to carry the first colour over the second colour yarn and then put to the back of the work, before putting the second colour over the hook and completing the stitch.

Where a pattern requires several different colours, using a bobbin for each colour will avoid a tangle of yarns. Bobbins are also useful when you are working a solid block in a second colour; stripes for example. In both cases, the yarns must be twisted together at the change of colours to avoid holes if the change is other than at the end of a row.

When changing colours during a row of trebles, with the wrong side of the work facing, keep the last two loops on the hook. Bring the first colour to the front of the work, put the second colour yarn over the hook and complete the stitch. Where several stitches form the pattern, carry the first colour over the second colour yarn and then work the stitch in the second colour yarn.

If you are working half trebles, change the yarn before drawing through the three loops on the hook. If you are working double crochet, change the yarn before drawing through the two loops on the hook.

READING PATTERN INSTRUCTIONS

Pattern instructions give the number of chains to be worked to form the foundation chain. These will be given as a multiple of x; any number of odd or even stitches.

A multiple of x means that the number given is the number of stitches required to work that particular stitch which is then repeated for as many times as required to achieve the final measurement. So, if the pattern states a multiple of 4 + 1, then the number of stitches must be divisible by four plus one further stitch, excluding any chains for turning.

Crochet patterns use asterisks (*) in the same way as knitting patterns to show which part of the instructions should be repeated until the end of the row or until further instructions are given. An example would be:
row 1: * 1 dc in first st, 1 ch, miss 1 ch; rep from * ending with 1 dc in each last 2 sts.

Where more than one stitch is to be worked into a single stitch, this is indicated by the use of brackets and where this instruction is to be repeated, the number of times this has to be done is given after the end bracket. The * indicates the section of the instructions to be repeated and the end of that section is marked with either ; or *. Any instructions for the ending of the row follow this section, ending with the number of turning chains required for the next row. For example:
row 1: 1 tr in 3rd ch from hook, miss next 2 ch, * [(1 dc, 2 ch, 3 tr) in next st, miss 2 ch] twice, 1 tr in next st, miss 2 ch; rep from * ending with 1 tr in last ch, 2 turning ch.

SHAPING

All shaping is worked by adding or taking away a number of stitches to or from a row. The average row in crochet is much deeper than a knitting row, so special care must be taken to avoid an uneven edge when increasing or decreasing.

Many patterns give shaping instructions for decreasing by omitting the first and last stitches on a row, and for increasing by working twice into the first and last stitches on a row. However, this can produce an uneven edge which is awkward to seam when making up. There are better methods which give a neater finish (see below).

The number of stitches cast on for each garment piece is calculated to fit the pattern exactly. As soon as any shaping is required, the beginning and ends of pattern rows will change. Patterns made from basic stitches are fairly easy to cope with; you can see how to work each stitch, keeping the pattern correct as you increase or decrease from the stitches worked before. With more elaborate patterns, it is worth studying how the stitch works so that you can increase or decrease accordingly.

A row counter helps you to keep count of rows so that you know exactly which pattern row is being worked and when the next piece of shaping is due.

DECREASING

To decrease a number of stitches, work the required number of rows, omitting the turning chain at the end of the last row. On the following row, work the number of stitches to be fastened off in slip stitch, then work the turning chain (to count as the first stitch of this row), miss the first stitch from the hook and work in pattern to the end of the row.

If groups of stitches are to be fastened off at each end of the row, work as described above, then work in pattern to the required number of stitches from the end of the row. Work the turning chain and turn. If stitches are to be fastened off on the following row, omit the turning chain at the end of the row.

Some patterns will give individual decreasing instructions. Otherwise, to decrease a stitch, work the turning chain to count as the first stitch in the usual way, miss the second stitch, work in pattern to the last two stitches, miss the next stitch and work the last stitch, then work the turning chain.

If a long stitch, such as a double treble or triple treble, is being worked, an alternative method avoids a gap. In this method, the turning chain forms the first stitch. Work the second stitch in the normal way but omitting the last stage (two loops remain on the hook). Work the third stitch also omitting the last stage (three loops remain on the hook), yarn over hook, draw loop through all the loops on the hook [figs. 32–33]. For a two-stitch decrease, see figs. 34–35.

In this way, the second and third stitches become one stitch only at the top of the stitch giving the correct number of stitches for the following row; there is no gap left at the bottom of the stitches.

The same method can be used at the end of a row, taking the second and third from last stitch together and working the last stitch in the usual way.

INCREASING

To increase a number of stitches, work the required number of rows, omitting the turning chain at the end of the last row. Work a turning chain for the required number of stitches to be cast on, plus those for the turning chain, turn. Count the turning chain as the first stitch, work in the pattern across the other chain stitches and then to the end of the row.

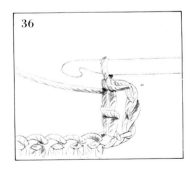

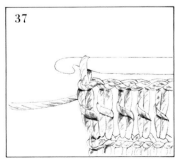

To increase a stitch, work the turning chain to count as the first stitch, then work two stitches in the second stitch (or stipulated stitch). At the end of a row, work two stitches in the last, or the last but one stitch working the last stitch in the usual way and work the turning chain to count as the first stitch of the next row [figs. 36 and 37].

BUTTONHOLES

Buttonholes may be worked to be vertical or horizontal. To make a vertical buttonhole, divide the work in two at the point where the buttonhole is to be worked and work each side separately. When it is the required depth, continue the work across both sections.

To make horizontal buttonholes, when working in double crochet, miss two (or more) stitches and work the equivalent number of chains. Work double crochet over the chain stitches on the next row.

As half trebles are deeper stitches, horizontal buttonholes are worked differently. At the beginning of the buttonhole, put the hook from top to bottom under the middle thread of the stitch just completed, yarn over hook, draw a loop through, yarn over hook and draw through two loops (this replaces the first chain). Continue with 1 chain, hook under left thread of previous stitch, yarn over hook and draw through a loop. Repeat this last instruction for the required width of the buttonhole. Finish the buttonhole by putting the hook under the thread to the left of the last stitch, yarn over hook, draw a loop through, miss the required number of stitches in previous row to correspond to the number of stitches worked for the buttonhole, put hook in next stitch, yarn over hook and draw a loop through, yarn over hook and draw through the three loops on the hook.

The method for working horizontal buttonholes in trebles is almost exactly the same. However, the hook for the first stitch is put under the first diagonal thread halfway down the last treble. Complete by drawing through a loop under the last diagonal thread, missing the required number of stitches in the previous row, hook into next stitch, yarn over hook, draw a loop through, yarn over hook and draw through two loops, yarn over hook and draw through remaining two loops. Continue in the pattern.

BUTTONS

Making crochet-covered buttons is simple. The foundation can be round a button mould, an inexpensive button or a metal ring.

Round buttons are worked as follows:
Work 3 ch and join with a sl st.
1st round: 6 dc in circle, join with a sl st to first st.
2nd round: 2 dc in each st of previous round, join with a sl st to first st.
3rd round: 1 dc into each st, join with a sl st into first st.
Repeat 3rd round until foundation ring or button is covered.
Last round: * miss 1 dc, 1 dc in next st; repeat from * to end, join with a sl st into first st.

Slip crochet cover over button and draw together underneath, leaving an end of yarn for sewing it on to the garment.

To make ring buttons, work a round of double crochet closely all round the ring, join with a slip stitch to the first stitch. Work strands of yarn diagonally across the back of the ring and sew the button to the garment through the centre of these strands.

SEAMS

Use the original yarn and a blunt-ended wool needle for sewing garment pieces together. If the yarn is not suitable, use a 3 or 4 ply yarn in the same shade.

BACKSTITCH SEAM

Place the two pieces right right sides together. Join in the yarn by making three small running stitches over each other, one stitch in from the edge. Put the needle back into the

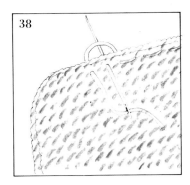
38

beginning of the running stitch and pull the yarn through. Insert the needle from the back, allowing a gap the length of a small running stitch and pull the yarn through [fig. 38]. Repeat this along the seam, keeping the stitches neat and even and one stitch in from the edge of both garment pieces. Take care not to split the worked stitches. This method is firm, yet elastic, keeps the garment in shape and will not break even when fairly roughly treated.

CROCHETED SEAM

The seams of garments made from an even pattern, such as double crochet, half treble or treble crochet, may be joined by slip stitch [fig. 39] or a single row of double crochet [fig. 40]. Take care to ensure that the seam is the same length as the finished garment and that it has not been stretched or pulled too tightly.

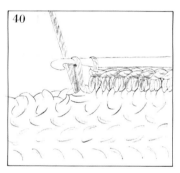

WOVEN FLAT SEAM

Open patterns will require a woven flat seam to bring the two edges together without forming a ridge. Place the right sides together and put your finger between the two pieces to be joined. Insert the needle from the front through both pieces below the corresponding

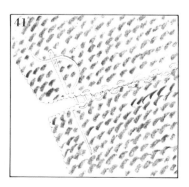

'pips', pull the yarn through. Insert the needle from the back through both pieces, allowing a gap the length of a small running stitch and pull the yarn through. The seam will then be drawn together and will be neat and flat when pressed [fig. 41]. This method is always used for ribbing and very fine garments.

DECORATIVE SEAM

When a firm stitch has been worked, lapped seams can be used on yokes and square set sleeves. Place the garment pieces right sides together, with the underneath part projecting 125 mm [½ inch] beyond the edge of the upper part. Backstitch along the edge. Turn to the right side and backstitch 125 mm [½ inch] from the first seam through both thicknesses, taking care to keep the line of stitching even and straight.

SHOULDER SEAMS

Backstitch firmly one stitch in from the edge, taking the stitching across the 'steps' of the shaping in a straight line. Press on the wrong side. Reinforce the seams of heavy garments with ribbon or tape. Where a shoulder seam is straight, a flat or crocheted seam can also be used.

SET-IN SLEEVES

Mark the centre top of the sleeve and pin it in position to the shoulder seam. Pin the fastened off stitches to the fastened off stitches of the body. Keeping the sleeve smooth on either side of the shoulder seam, work a fine backstitch around the curves as near to the edge as possible or, where suitable, a flat seam.

SIDE AND SLEEVE SEAMS

Join with backstitch in one complete seam as near to the edge as possible or, where suitable, a flat seam.

COLLARS

Matching centre backs, place the right side of the collar to the wrong side of the neck. Take care not to stretch the neckline. Oversew or join with a firm backstitch as near the edge as possible.

SEWN-ON BANDS

To join bands worked separately to a garment, use a woven flat seam, matching row for row.

SEWN-ON POCKETS

Use a slip stitch to attach sewn-on pockets or any applied bands or decoration [fig. 42]. Be careful to keep the line absolutely straight. A good way to do this is to thread a fine, double-pointed knitting needle under every alternate stitch of the line to be followed and catch one stitch from the edge of the pocket and one stitch from the needle alternately.

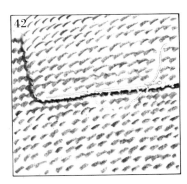

SKIRT WAIST

Cut elastic to the size required and join the ends to form a circle. Mark both the waistline

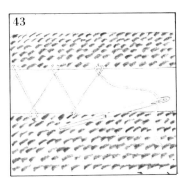

of the skirt and the elastic into quarter sections and pin the elastic into position on the wrong side. Take care to work evenly. Hold the work over the fingers of the left hand and, with the elastic slighly stretched, work a herringbone stitch, catching the elastic above and below [fig. 43].

RIBBON FACINGS

If possible, lightly press the part to be faced, being careful not to stretch the edge. Use soft ribbon for facings.

Ribbon for facing buttonhole bands should be wide enough to cover the strip plus an allowance of 60-125 mm [$\frac{1}{4}$-$\frac{1}{2}$ inch] on each side and a 125 mm [$\frac{1}{2}$ inch] hem at the top and bottom. Be very careful not to stretch the crochet when measuring the ribbon lengths. Cut the facings for both the buttonhole and button bands at the same time so that they match exactly.

Fold in the turnings and pin the ribbon to the wrong side, easing the crochet evenly. Using matching thread, slip stitch with very tiny stitches along all edges. Cut buttonholes against the straight grain of the ribbon, remembering to make them wide enough for the buttons. Oversew the ribbon and crochet together to avoid fraying. Neaten by working buttonhole stitch with the original yarn.

Grosgrain ribbon can be shaped to fit a curved edge by pressing with a hot iron and gently stretching the edge until the desired curve has been made.

When facing two edges at right angles, seam the outside edge in place first, then fold the ribbon in a mitred corner. Seam the inside edge.

SEWING IN ZIP FASTENERS

Pin the zip fastener to the opening, taking care not to stretch the crochet. Sew in place using backstitch, keeping the grain of the crochet straight. Except on very heavy garments, nylon zip fasteners are better because of their lightness and flexibility.

HINTS ON WORKING CROCHET

After casting on the foundation chain and working the first row, it can be infuriating to discover that you have miscounted and that there are too few chains in the base chain to finish correctly. One way to pre-empt this problem is to leave a long tail of yarn when you make the initial slip knot. Then, if necessary, you can use this to make good the missing number of chains.

A standard chart for turning chains is given under METHODS OF WORKING CROCHET. However, you should remember that the number of chains required can alter, depending on hook size, the type of yarn and the stitch being used. Sometimes fewer or more chains may be needed.

When the turning chain counts as the first stitch of a row, make sure that a stitch is worked at the end of the row into the top of the turning chain of the previous row. When a turning chain does not count as a first stitch, then remember to work the first stitch and not to work the stitch into the top of the turning chain.

Edges are neater if you miss the first stitch on each row. The appropriate turning chain takes its place and at the end, one stitch is worked into the turning chain.

It is sensible to count the number of stitches being worked from time to time to ensure that none has been lost.

When joining yarn in the middle of a row, put the hook into a stitch just before the join needs to be made. Loop the new yarn over and pull yarn through, then continue with the new yarn. If the pattern being worked is a solid design, you can join the new yarn by laying it across the top of the work and working stitches over it. Then continue the work in the new yarn, laying the remnant of the previous yarn along the top of the work and working stitches over it.

If pieces have to be sewn together at the finish of the work and if the yarn is suitable for seaming, leave a generous amount of yarn after fastening off. This can then be used for sewing the seams.

Foundation chains may tend to draw in the bottom of the work. One way to avoid this is to work the base chain with a hook one size larger or with doubled yarn. An alternative is to work a rather more solid foundation chain than a simple chain. After making the first loop, work 2 ch, hook into first loop, * yoh, draw a loop through, yoh and draw it through the 2 loops on the hook; repeat from * to end, putting the hook each time into the thread at left.

Newcomers to crochet will find it easier if they start with a pattern using a large hook and thick yarn. The approved way to crochet is described under GETTING STARTED, but some people find this difficult. It may be easier to wind the yarn round the right hand, hold the hook in the right hand and work the stitch using the right hand. The left hand is used to hold the work. Although unorthodox, this method suits some people better.

Left-handed crocheters can use the diagrams in this book by following them in reverse. Simply prop the book open with the appropriate page facing a mirror.

To identify the right and wrong side of the work, look for the end of yarn at the beginning of the foundation chain. It will be at the left-hand edge when the right side is facing, provided that the first row worked was a right side row.

YARN SPINNERS

Avocet
Hammerain House
Hookstone Avenue
Harrogate
North Yorkshire HG2 8ER.

Coats
Domestic Marketing Division
39 Durham Street
Glasgow G41 1BS.

DMC
through:
Dunlicraft
Pullman Road
Wigston
Leicester LE8 2DY.

Emu
Leeds Road
Greengates
Bradford
West Yorkshire BD10 9TE.

Jaeger and Patons
McMullen Road
Darlington
Co. Durham DL1 1YH.

Phildar
4 Gambrel Road
Westgate Industrial Estate
Northampton NN5 5NF.

Pingouin
Station House
81-83 Fulham High Street
London SW6 3JW.

Robin
Robin Mills
Idle
Bradford
West Yorkshire BD10 9TE.

Rowan
Green Lane Mill
Holmfirth
West Yorkshire HD7 1RW.

Sirdar
Flanshaw Lane
Alvethorpe
Wakefield
Yorkshire WF2 9ND.

Spectrum
Bankwell Road
Milnsbridge
Huddersfield
Yorkshire HD3 4LU.

H.G. Twilley
Roman Mill
Stamford
Lincolnshire PE9 1BG.

Wendy
Carter & Parker
Gordon Mills
Guiseley
Leeds LS20 9BD.

ACKNOWLEDGEMENTS

Women's clothes: Nicole Farhi; men's clothes: Paul Smith and French Connection; jewellery: Butler & Wilson; shoes: Maud Frizon; tights: Sock Shop; watches: models' own; scarves: stylist's own.

Hair: Derek Thompson at Michaeljohn
Make-up: Pierre La Roche at JRB Associates
Models: Kelly Brennan, Lisa Dolan, Virginia Young, Nick Bourn, Andrew Cote, Martin Reynolds at The Edge.

Photographed at Milton Manor House near Abingdon-on-Thames, Oxfordshire, England. Open to the public.

Additional photography by Rachel Andrew
Illustrations by Studio Briggs

This book would not have been possible without the generous help of many. The original pattern research was done by Susan Wallace. Particular thanks are due to Avocet, DMC, Coats, Emu, Pingouin, Robin, Rowan, Sirdar, Spectrum, Twilleys and Wendy for re-working the original patterns; to Jaeger, Patons and Phildar for supplying yarn.
Individual crocheters did sterling work in producing the garments and my thanks go to Lena Baker, Polly Cox, Pauline Fitzpatrick and Sheila Wrixson for their fine work.
My thanks must go too to Alex Kroll for his guidance throughout.